On Work and Leadership

THE RSA

The Royal Society for the encouragement of Arts, Manufactures and Commerce (RSA) was founded in 1754 with a mission to 'embolden enterprise, to enlarge science, to refine art, to improve our manufactures and to extend our commerce'. Believing that a thriving economy was the determining factor in the development of a civilized society, the RSA's founding Fellows sought to encourage innovation, the acquisition of new skills and the creation of new markets.

The RSA today uses its independence and the resources of its international Fellowship to stimulate debate, develop ideas and encourage action in its main fields of interest: business and industry, design and technology, education, the arts and the environment. The RSA Fellowship (now numbering nearly 21,500 in the UK and abroad) is drawn from almost every vocation and provides a resource of expertise and practical experience on which the Society can call.

The RSA is good at forming partnerships, at working with others to increase the pressure for change. The Society provides a forum for discussion within which ideas may be shaped and action stimulated. Often the process starts with a lecture, seminar or conference, then may follow active promotion through a project, campaign or award scheme.

Current projects include Redefining Schooling, PROJECT 2001, Focus on Food, Forum for Ethics in the Workplace, the RSA Student Design Awards, and The Arts Matter programme (see also the back pages of this book).

For more information please write to The Director, RSA, 8 John Adam Street, London WC2N 6EZ or telephone 0171 930 5115. (Fax 0171 839 5805, Website http://www.rsa.org.uk)

RSA

ON WORK
AND LEADERSHIP

A selection of lectures organized by the
Royal Society for the encouragement of
Arts, Manufactures and Commerce

Gower

Published by
Gower Publishing Limited
Gower House
Croft Road
Aldershot
Hampshire GU11 3HR
England

Gower
Old Post Road
Brookfield
Vermont 05036
USA

British Library in Cataloguing Publication Data
A catalogue record for this book is available from the British Library.

ISBN 0-566-08108-3

Lecture sponsors: Andersen Consulting, The EMI Group, Diageo plc, Deloitte & Touche, KPMG, Comino Foundation.

Text designed by Bob Vickers and David Brown and printed in Great Britain at the University Press, Cambridge.

CONTENTS

FOREWORD

On my first day at work, long ago now, I was presented with two documents – a description of the company's pension scheme and an example of the course of the career I might expect with it up to retirement, including information that the average expectation of life after retirement was 18 months! That was typical then of what many expected of the job, of the organization and of responsible leadership – the guarantee of what was, literally, a job for life.

All has changed now. Jobs, businesses and leaders all need re-definition in an age where 'distance is dead', where people are truly the only assets and where 'command and control' no longer works as a method of leadership. We badly need some clues to the new future, some examples of what works and some lessons from organizations other than business who have to struggle with their own changing worlds.

This collection of essays provides all three. They offer the outlines of a map for the journey that all businesses are already committed to, however unwillingly or unexpectedly, a journey to a new and, just possibly, a better world. Appropriately for a busy audience they are short, wonderfully readable and pleasingly provocative. Personally, I am delighted that the essays had their origin in the RSA, which is once again living up to its aim to stimulate thought and action in pursuit of a better society.

Charles Handy

Charles Handy is a past Chairman of the Society.

INTRODUCTION

The world of work is changing. Technology and increasing globalization are affecting the roles of organizations and individuals. Companies' understanding of the factors leading to sustainable corporate success are also changing in a way which can accommodate important ethical issues.

In the UK the Royal Society for the encouragement of Arts, Manufactures and Commerce, founded in 1754 by William Shipley 'to embolden enterprise, to enlarge science, to refine art, to improve our manufactures and to extend our commerce' has for many years been an agent of change, stimulating debate through its annual programme of lectures and setting change in motion through a range of specific programmes and projects (see page 139).

This book consists of a selection of RSA lectures, printed in edited versions, by leading commentators and practitioners. Relating to work, corporate change, working ethics and leadership, they cover key areas which the RSA has championed and which have frequently developed into sustained RSA projects and initiatives. Together they represent key corporate preoccupations and offer insight into how progress can be made, problems solved and new models developed to overcome conflicting pressures and demands that beset organizations and their people. In featuring organizations in sectors ranging from the police (page 57) to the financial sector (page 85), and from legal partnerships (page 95) to the health service (page 115) they also show how unlikely connections can be made and how different sectors can learn from each other.

The book begins by exploring the issues relating to the individual in today's working environment, the implications of working on one's own and changing working cultures. In his Redefining Work lecture the American author William Bridges looks at the meaning of 'jobs' and suggests that it no longer makes sense to think in such terms. The trend is towards paying for output and input for work that needs to be done rather than 'jobs', which could have positive implications for otherwise excluded social groups such as the disabled, against whom fixed job structures too often discriminate.

Professor Cary Cooper, a leading expert on stress management, explores the psychological implications of changing work patterns, and the effects on both the individual and family life. How will companies manage flexible teleworkers? Will women, more used to irregular work patterns than men, cope better with part-time working as people face up to the employment insecurity caused by downsizing and technology? How will we adapt to the short-term contract culture and can there be a way of making work more fulfilling?

In the Deloitte & Touche Lecture, Frances Cairncross from *The Economist* describes the negative and positive changes resulting from the technological revolution. 'The death of distance' brings new opportunities for companies and individuals to access the global marketplace. The vastly reduced cost of transporting ideas and services will have an impact on all institutions, both corporate and governmental, with new implications for productivity and the distribution of power, and a greater emphasis on the value of knowledge.

The world is getting smaller for companies and individuals, but what does this mean for corporate citizenship? In his lecture David Logan from the Corporate Citizenship Company examines how transnational companies with 'populations' larger than some countries exert an increasing influence on states in the post-Communist era and how they address issues of corporate responsibility. Today they are called to account by the moral authority of increasingly influential not-for-profit organizations, while the state is taking on a new role in society of setting social and environmental targets for business, then monitoring and measuring its performance against them.

Sheena Carmichael, whose lecture was delivered to the RSA's Forum for Ethics in the Workplace, is concerned that people at work should be able to practise the same kind of values that they practise in their private lives. She explains how ethical audits can help companies not only to act more ethically but also to improve productivity and can therefore be of benefit to all stakeholders.

The second Forum for Ethics in the Workplace lecture by Richard Wells, former Chief Constable of South Yorkshire, explains how in the police force quantitative, statistically-judged success in detecting crimes can mean failure in the ethical sense and lead to the potential for wrong and the undermining of public confidence, as it can in other public sector services such as health and education. He describes ways in which organizations can take a more ethical, democratic approach, aiming at a position in which people sustain achievement voluntarily because they are valued. Cultural changes introducing trust, openness and innovation will result in real, qualitative success.

A more ethical approach to employees forms part of the inclusive approach advocated in the RSA's *Tomorrow's Company* report (see page 75), the outcome of the RSA Tomorrow's Company Inquiry, which re-examined the sources of sustainable business success. In the first of four Tomorrow's Company lectures included in this book Sir Stuart Hampson, chairman of John Lewis Partnership, relates the history of its partnership philosophy and illustrates how the way in which it manages its staff – its 'partners' – involving them in shaping the company and in profit-sharing, has been a major contributor to the Partnership's success and long-term strength.

In 'Tomorrow's Company – A Journey of Discovery', Nick

Obolensky, chief executive of Tomorrow's Company Enterprises, explains how ten diverse companies, brought together through the Pathfinder Project, were able to progress along the path to the inclusive approach to business. The experience of two of the companies involved in the project, Osborne Clarke and Birmingham Midshires, are described in the two responding lectures which follow.

According to Mike Jackson, former chief executive of Birmingham Midshires, strong leadership is the glue which holds everything together. The book concludes with six views on leadership, specifically on the leadership of organizations and the question of whether leadership can be taught. In the first of these Professor Gareth Jones analyses the Western concept of leadership in the historical context of rational and moral thought, explaining the evolution of leadership theories and exploring key leadership qualities. In the two responding lectures Hilary Cropper of the F.I. Group emphasizes how leaders must galvanize staff with a unifying purpose, establishing a set of shared beliefs and common objectives which encourage a collective desire to succeed; and Helen Taylor Thompson of Mildmay Hospital exemplifies the personal leadership qualities of persuasion, motivation and energetic individuality in her description of how she ensured that Mildmay survived and grew to be a world leader in its field.

Answering the question of whether leadership qualities can be taught, General Jack Deverell emphasizes the importance of 'the being' as well as 'the doing': 'Once we start to delve into being rather than doing, we are confronted by intangible and perhaps unfashionable concepts of duty, service, example, motivation and so on. These virtues lie at the heart of effective leadership.' He concludes that these less tangible leadership qualities are difficult to teach and sometimes impossible.

Responding to General Deverell's lecture, Philip Hodgson develops the theme of training and learning further, putting forward the theory that strong leadership involves 'difficult learning' –

meeting difficult challenges, facing up to hard lessons and tackling difficult tasks and situations that one would prefer to avoid. Lastly, the Olympic swimmer, Adrian Moorhouse, adds his own interpretations and insight, drawn from the world of sport, to those of the two previous lecturers.

In covering a range of views on a range of topics from different experts and sectors the book provides an overview of key factors affecting the business world and the individual. It demonstrates how these factors can be managed with better principles and new models of both ethical and productive best practice to bring longer-lasting rewards both for the company and the individual.

The RSA would like to thank the lecturers and sponsors who supported the RSA 1997/98 lecture programme on which this book is based.

Redefining Work – Creating You and Company

WILLIAM BRIDGES

Author

My original training was not in business or in organizational matters – it was as a literary and social historian. My present work results from a career shift, and much of my sense of what changing one's work identity and changing one's working life involve comes from my own experience. My own professional origins explain my particular way of approaching questions: it always seems useful to say 'how will this look when it is a matter of history?' – to imagine that we are looking back at present changes from, say, the year 2050. What are people likely to be saying about those changes?

The period 1840 to 1990 could truly be called the age of the job. By 'job' I mean a set area of responsibility. The employment is open-ended but long-term and it fits within an organizational structure, occupying a fixed place with set hours. Usually there is a single boss or somebody who is in charge of one's activity and a set and fairly narrow band of salary that goes with the job – one can receive pay rises but one would have to be promoted out of that job to get a significantly greater amount of money. The job, in this definition, is the access to a series of stepping stones of promotion or advancement.

This definition relates to the archetypal job to which most of us were exposed by parents and teachers, but not all jobs fall into those categories. Before 1840 people didn't have fixed positions. They worked hard but nobody set their hours or paid them a salary. There were all kinds of work arrangements but no jobs in today's meaning of the word. The job as we know it is a historical artefact created by a particular social order.

When this current period is seen retrospectively we are going to think that jobs in that sense ended at the beginning of the 1990s. One view is that machinery has come along and swallowed up all the significant work. I don't share that view. There's an enormous amount of work to be done but nobody has been able to box it up into these things called jobs. We say there's no work to be done when what we mean is 'there are no jobs'.

Another, more dysfunctional view sees 'good jobs' disappearing, going overseas or being taken by machinery. They are giving way to redundancy, temporary workers and outsourcing. You would think that during the good times which we have experienced recently, when the unemployment rate in the UK has been 5.5 per cent and in the US a little lower, people ought to be comfortable, but clearly they are not. Why is this?

Different patterns of employment
Here are some current scenarios which demonstrate the move towards different patterns of employment.

In New York, until the last recession, bank economists could earn six-figure salaries. Then several key economists left employment and set up small firms which sold economic forecasts for no more than $2,000. Will a senior executive of a bank hire a full-time, long-term economist and pay $150,000, or spend $2,000 for a consensus forecast of some of the best economists in America?

Carter's Gold Medal soft drinks company in the UK had a distribution problem. They did not, however, fire the head of distribution and bring in a new executive but brought in a temporary, albeit a skilled temporary, with executive experience in distribution. He approached the issue the way a consultant would, studied it and made recommendations. The company hired him to implement his recommendations. He thus became a temporary worker. When he had saved £1.5 million out of a £6 million budget he hired his replacement and left. What kind of worker is that? That's a peculiar worker, acting as a consultant, working like a temp and then hiring a replacement.

The World Trade Center in New York City was blown up in 1993 by a terrorist bomb. The company that won the bid to clean it up was from Norcross, Georgia, and had 60 employees. It hired temporary workers until it had 3,600 employees and the job took only 16 days, two of which were lost to a blizzard.

For the past 15 years Intel has been one of the most successful companies in the US. People don't have 'jobs' at Intel, they're on cross-functional teams: they're trained to do each other's work – they don't talk about 'jobs', they talk about 'assignments'.

These scenarios show that organizations are deciding, for a variety of reasons, that the full-time, long-term job is no longer the best way to get work done. You could say things are falling apart so 'Let's put Humpty Dumpty together again'. That is what most governments are saying: 'How are we going to create more jobs?' To my way of thinking that's like saying, 'How are we going to put more deckchairs on the deck of the Titanic?'

Jobs today are proving to be relatively inflexible and unresponsive to changing conditions. Job-based attitudes don't work in fast-moving companies. People keep doing their jobs, rather than doing the work that needs to be done.

Jobs also distort accountability. We like to think that jobs nail accountability down, that if we have somebody in that job we will see that it gets done, but in fact jobs can work quite differently. Some years ago San Diego Zoo went through a re-engineering process and removed traditional jobs, replacing them with cross-functional teams, in which people worked together without spelled-out, distinct responsibilities. The head of the Employee

Department at that time commented on the major change:

> 'When I joined the zoo my job was as a groundsman, and a
> groundsman's job is to go around and pick up the trash in the
> public areas... But whenever I was tired, if I saw a popcorn
> box out there I went up to it and I kicked it sideways, because
> if I could get it under a bush it was the gardener's job, not
> mine.'

That seems to me a very profound story: one of the things that jobs,
in that sense, encouraged was fighting over work.

Jobs create fragile identities – teacher, machinist, waitress – but
would not have done so in a period when there were other things
to give us identity. In a fragmented society jobs are a solid source
of identity – or they were. These are the things that are wrong
with jobs.

One of the changes that has happened recently is the rise of
knowledge work. Another is that output has become increasingly
customized so we don't have long production runs that allow us
to cut up the work into pieces. The time and place focus that
the job required has been badly undermined by communications
technology. Yet our educational system continues to prepare people
for jobs, and trade unions are working to protect jobs. Someone
looking back from the year 2050 will say that this was a schizo-
phrenic time with people desperately clinging on to a social institution that was being destroyed by the forces of change.

Demand for organizational change
What needs to be done? First, organizations need to rethink major
parts of their policies, structures, cultural norms and roles. They
need to think about de-jobbing pay. Pay is going to move more
towards output. Some firms already pay this way in the form of
bonuses for output and profit-sharing: 65 per cent of American
firms use some form of variable pay now.

Another tendency is pay for increased capability, sometimes

called competency-based pay, when people are paid more if they bring increased skills to the job. This tendency tries to increase the input into the job; the former tries to increase the output from the job. Simply paying people to do jobs may be paying them not to contribute, not to add value.

The de-jobbed organization is also going to change its performance management. 'What are the expected outcomes for you in the next two months?' That question would have meant little to the nineteenth-century factory worker but means a great deal today at companies such as Intel or Microsoft. At Intel, where people are on changing teams, there is no one manager who can evaluate output, so they have a system for collecting evaluations from customers and integrating those into a single evaluation.

De-jobbing has implications for hiring, which used to take experience and education more seriously than cutting-edge companies do today. An American company making Web page software got a hit on their Web page from a fellow who said, 'I do your kind of work and I'd like you to go to Web page so-and-so, have a look at what I do and see if you'd be interested in it.' His Web page was more sophisticated than anything anybody in the company could do, so they contacted him and said, 'We'd like to talk with you about the possibility of employment. Can you come in tomorrow?' He replied that he couldn't come till Saturday, 'because my mom can't drive me.' (He was 13 years old!)

Education still means a tremendous amount because skill and knowledge are essential for this kind of work, but this is not education as we usually understand it. More people are being hired without the traditional degrees, without the traditional experience.

Forbes Magazine was looking for an editorial assistant. They didn't ask applicants about their experience but brought a group of them into a room and said, 'We're going to send you on a treasure hunt. We want you to find the following three items: a first edition of an Evelyn Waugh novel; the best price on a yacht charter in the Caribbean; and the unlisted phone numbers of three celebrities.'

The applicants were bemused at first, then one of them jumped up and ran out of the door. A few others followed but the rest stayed there wondering what in the world was happening. The one who ran out had realized that this was a test. The company was interested in whether they could do the job of an editorial assistant. What better way to discover that than to set up such a test situation?

The future of trade unions
It is clear that there are changes ahead for unions. They are going to find it harder to concentrate just on job protection as their business, but a whole new purpose for unions is advocacy, worker development, helping workers buy the kinds of services they need but can't buy singly. There are existing models for this future role: the National Union of Journalists in Britain is a good example because it is made up of freelancers as well as employees, and in the US there is another example, the Screenwriters' Guild. However, not enough unions have moved in this direction of serving the needs of the independent worker.

Schools have a whole new agenda. There has been a considerable move in the US back toward basic skills. Whenever there's any printed list of the abilities that workers need it always starts with reading, writing, listening, speaking, working together, leading. It turns out that in spite of the fact that we are this sophisticated twenty-first century society with new needs, the abilities people require are still the same.

Creative problem-solving and self-knowledge should be added to the list, because tomorrow's worker is going to operate more like an independent small company than a traditional employee – whether or not the person is employed – so self-knowledge is going to be important. In my book, *Creating You & Co*, there's a whole sequence of self-knowledge exercises built around the acronym DATA: Desires, Abilities, Temperament, Assets – the incidental things that happen to be true of you.[1]

Workers need help in understanding themselves. You used not

to have to understand yourself; you used simply to have to take the courses you needed for a job. Now it is important to know who you are and what you bring to the table. In the US, and in the UK also, much education is being reformatted as problem-centred or project-centred. That's a hopeful sign because one of the shocks that individuals have in moving from university to work is that after learning sequences of things that are well organized, they are plunged into a work situation and just given a problem.

New institutions need to develop; we are seeing the beginning of a kind of temporary agency that is more like an employer, but what about agents? Writers and actors have them, and some independent workers could certainly use them. In the US, software writers are using agents, and we will see more of them as time goes on. In some ways an executive search professional is an agent, although we haven't defined them that way. We already have information brokers who tell people where jobs are; workers now need people to tell them about organizations' unmet needs that are not in the form of jobs.

Areas of growth
We need new institutions as part of the solution to our problem and as a source of opportunity. Employment in traditional firms will not grow nearly as fast as the employment of the interface between the worker and these firms.

In this emerging world people will need to see that Desire, Ability, Temperament and Assets (DATA) can be built into something new. This can be done through a five-step process:

- The first step is examining your resources.
- The second step is to look at the markets round you: anywhere that there is an identifiable unmet need is a market.
- The third step is coming up with a product, something you can sell. Many workers have thought that their company had a product but that they did not. Today's workplace is

going to require people to be clearer about their products. What are you proposing to deliver? What will it do? Why is it better than somebody else's product?

- The fourth step is defining your business in the sense of what you do for people. Do you solve problems? Do you save money?

- Finally, you need a business plan, but not the sort produced for big businesses to raise money. Outline what you propose to do, why it's a good thing to do and why you should do it rather than somebody else – you will have to convince somebody to pay you money for doing it.

The approach that I am outlining may seem like one more way in which the haves are going to win out at the expense of the have-nots. In fact, it gives a second chance to many people who have not been favoured in the jobs world. When I gave a talk to a group of the President's Commission for the Handicapped in the US, I was worried that they were going to say, 'It's fine for you to talk about this brave new world for people who can see and walk well, who aren't deaf, and so on.' They said just the opposite: 'It's jobs that discriminate against us. If we could go to an employer and make an employment proposal where we spelled out what our product was and how it would benefit the employer to buy it – that is, to hire us to do something – it would be a tremendous advantage.' So the idea that the world I'm talking about is good only for the favoured is wrong. On the contrary, it may level the playing field.

Someone looking back at our age from the year 2050 is going to say, 'In 1997 they were in the closing days of the age of the job. Jobs stayed around for quite a while just the way agriculture stays around today, something that a minority of people do and the rest of us benefit from.' If you particularly like agriculture, it's still a good sector to go into. That will always be an option; but in the years to come organizations will begin to realign themselves so that they aren't job-based, so that people do the work that needs doing instead of just their jobs. Governments will change policies. Education will begin to prepare young people for a world which isn't boxed up into jobs. Unions will rethink their own purpose for being. New institutions will come into play to help us. We're going to find ourselves in a world in which jobs do not matter the way they do today, in which people have a variety of ways of getting work done and being paid for getting work done, and employment doesn't necessarily mean a whole-time, long-term job.

Reference
1   Bridges, W. (1998) *Creating You & Co*, New York/London: HarperCollins.

THE CHANGING NATURE OF WORK – TOWARDS SHORT-TERM CONTRACT CULTURES

PROFESSOR CARY COOPER

BUPA Professor of Organizational Psychology and Health,
Manchester School of Management
and
Pro Vice Chancellor, UMIST

More organizations are downsizing, market-testing and outsourcing, which means more of us in the future will be selling our services to organizations on short-term contract or freelance bases. What are the implications for the wealth of the individual, his or her family and future organizations? Can individuals commit to organizations that don't commit to them? Can families survive the conflicts surrounding the changing role of men and women? Will women become the main breadwinners, given their flexible approach to work? Will these developments create 'virtual organizations' with more teleworkers?

The 1960s epitomized the limitless possibilities of change, as society confronted the horrors of the Vietnam War and the traditional and established lifestyles of the post-war period. It was an era that embraced new technology, with UK Prime Minister Harold Wilson proclaiming that the 'white heat of technology' was about to transform our lives, producing a leisure age of 20-hour weeks. This was followed by the 1970s period of industrial strife, conflict and retrenchment. The workplace became the battle ground between employers and workers, between the middle classes and the working classes, between liberal and conservative thinking. This industrial confrontation was highlighted by Studs Terkel in his acclaimed book of the period *Working*:

> Work is by its very nature about violence – to the spirit as well as to the body. It is about ulcers as well as accidents, about shouting matches as well as fistfights, about nervous break-downs as well as kicking the dog around. It is, above all, about daily humiliations. To survive the day is triumph enough for the walking wounded among the great many of us.[1]

Out of the turmoil of the 1970s came the 'enterprise culture' of the 1980s, a decade of privatizations, statutory constraints on industrial relations, mergers and acquisitions, strategic alliances, joint ventures, process re-engineering and the like, transforming workplaces into free market, hot-house cultures. Although this entrepreneurial period improved our economic competitiveness at home and in international markets, there were also the first signs of strain, as 'stress' and 'burnout' became concepts in the everyday vocabulary of many working people.

By the end of the 1980s and into the early 1990s, the sustained recession, together with the privatizing mentality regarding the public sector during the decade, laid the groundwork for potentially the most profound changes in the workplace since the industrial revolution. The early years of the 1990s were dominated by the effects of recession and efforts to get out of it, as organizations 'downsized', 'delayered', 'flattened' or 'right-sized'. Whatever euphemism you care to use, the hard reality experienced by many was job loss and constant change. There were fewer people, doing more work and feeling more job insecure. The rapid expansion of information technology also meant the added burden of informa-tion overload and the accelerating pace of work, with people demanding more and more information, and quicker and quicker. From the middle 1980s throughout the 1990s, we also saw the massive increase of women in the workplace, with a noticeable pushing (not shattering) of the glass ceiling further upwards. The changing role of men and women at work and at home added another dimension to the enormity of change taking place in the offices, factory floors and techno-cultures of UK Plc.[2]

The changing workplace
The downsizing and the rapidity of change has certainly taken its toll in the 1990s, particularly in the UK, where the restructuring of industry has outpaced our European partners. An International Survey Research (ISR) survey published in 1995, of 400 companies in 17 countries employing over 8 million workers throughout Europe, found that over the last ten years the UK's employee satisfaction level dropped from 64 per cent in 1985 to 53 per cent by 1995, the biggest drop of any European country.[3]

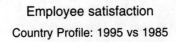

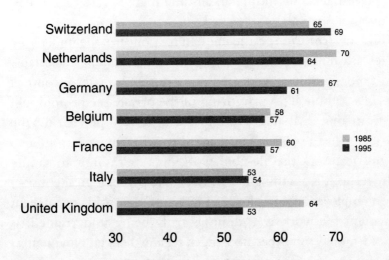

Figure 1: Relative employee satisfaction levels in different European countries (Source: ISR[3])

These changes also had effects on the family, as more and more two-earner families or couples emerged in a climate which was anything but 'family friendly'. The BT Forum's report on *The Cost of Communication Breakdown* found that by 1991 the UK had the highest divorce rate in Europe with over 171,000 divorces, while the proportion of people living in one parent families increased four fold between 1961 and 1991 – with the prediction that over 3 million children and young people will grow up in step families by the year 2000.[4]

This is in no small measure partly a result of a 'long working hours' culture in most public and private sector organizations in the UK. DEMOS's report, *Time Squeeze*, in 1995 found that 25 per cent of British male employees worked more than 48 hours a week; a fifth of all manual workers worked more than 50 hours; one in eight managers worked more than 60-hour weeks and seven out of ten British workers want to work a 40-hour week but only three out of ten do. In addition, the sickness absence rates rose during much of this period, recently hitting an all time high of £12 billion cost to industry in one year.[5]

While this scenario is cause enough for concern, the underlying trend toward outsourcing and market testing is leading inexorably toward a more insidious work environment, the short-term contract or freelance culture. This privatizing of the private sector no doubt stems from our insatiable appetite for massively privatizing the public sector in the 1980s. This has led to what employers refer to euphemistically as 'the flexible workforce', although in family friendly terms it is anything but flexible. The psychological contract between employer and employee in terms of 'reasonably permanent employment for work well done' is truly being undermined, as more and more employees no longer regard their employment as secure and many more are engaged in part-time working. From 1984 to 1994 the number of men working part time doubled, with the number of people employed by firms of more than 500 employees having slumped to just over a third of the employed population and with over one in eight British workers now self-employed.

There may be nothing inherently wrong with this trend, but a recent *Quality of Working Life* survey by the Institute of Management and UMIST (which has surveyed and will continue to survey 5,000 managers each year over the next five years) found some disturbing results among Britain's managers. First, organizations at the end of the 1990s were found to be in a state of constant change, with 61 per cent of this national sample of managers having undergone a major restructuring over the last 12 months.[6] The consequences of this change, even among a group supposedly in control of events, were increased job insecurity, lowered morale, and the erosion of motivation and loyalty.

Most of these changes involved downsizing, cost reduction, delayering and outsourcing. Yet the perception was that although these changes inevitably led to an increase in profitability and productivity, decision-making was slower and, more importantly, the organization was deemed to have lost the right mix of human resource skills and experience in the process. In addition, the impact

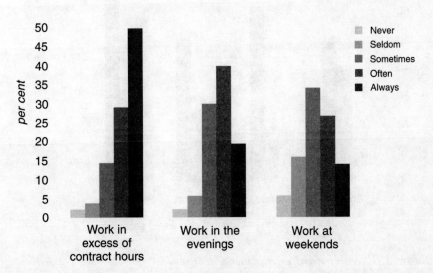

Figure 2: Working patterns, contract hours, evening and weekend work. (Source: Institute of Management[6])

on working patterns, contract hours and evening and weekend working was penal. It was found that 82 per cent of managers in the UK regularly work more than 40 hours a week, 38 per cent report working over 50-hour weeks and 41 per cent always or often work at weekends.

Poor communications and concerns about their future employability were some of the reasons for managers' insecurity. Sixty per cent of managers felt they were in the dark about their organization's future strategies, while 48 per cent say their biggest worry is financial security and employability in the wider job market. Because of the outsourcing and intrinsic job insecurity, 89 per cent of managers say they will need to develop new skills (such as IT, information management, financial management) over the next five years, presumably as they foresee the selling of their services to organizations on a freelance or short-term contract basis.

This snapshot of corporate life from Britain's managers high-

Figure 3: Effects of recent organizational change.
(Source: Institute of Management[6])

lights the likely destination of the workplace of the future. As Cooper and Jackson predict in their book *Creating Tomorrow's Organizations*, most organizations will have only a small core of full-time, permanent employees, working from a conventional office.[7] They will buy most of the skills they need on a contract basis, either from individuals working at home and linked to the company by computers and modems (teleworking), or by hiring people on short-term contracts to do specific jobs or carry out specific projects.

In this way companies will be able to maintain the flexibility they need to cope with a rapidly changing world. Much of this change is already happening, with BT claiming that more than 2.5 million people are already working wholly or partly from home and predicting this to rise to 4 million by the millennium. There is also a significant rise in the provision of interim management agencies to supply senior management on a project management basis to industry. All the trends are in the direction of what the Americans call the 'contingent workforce', an army of blue-collar, white-collar and managerial temps.

Consequences of change

So what are the consequences of this change?

First, as more and more people work from their home, whether part time or on a short-term contract, we will be increasingly creating 'virtual organizations'. The big corporate question here is 'how will this virtual organization of the future manage this dispersed workforce, with communications difficulties already apparent in existing organizational structures (as found by the IM–UMIST survey)?

Second, with two out of three families/couples two-earner or dual career, how will working from home affect the delicate balance between home and work or the shifting roles between men and women? Indeed, with employers increasingly looking for and recruiting 'flexible workers', won't women be preferred to men given their history of flexibility? For example, there are currently five times as many women working part time than men, and although twice as many men are now working part time than a decade ago, women are historically more experienced at discontinuous career patterns, flowing in and out of the labour market, working part time and on short-term contracts.

Third, since the industrial revolution many white-collar, managerial and professional workers have not experienced high levels of job insecurity. Even many blue-collar workers who were laid off in heavy manufacturing industries of the past were frequently re-employed when times got better. The question that society has to ask itself is: can human beings cope with permanent job insecurity, without the safety and security of organizational structures, which in the past provided training, development and careers? The European survey by ISR[3] provides some cause for concern in this regard, showing the UK as experiencing a decline in employee satisfaction in terms of employment security that is

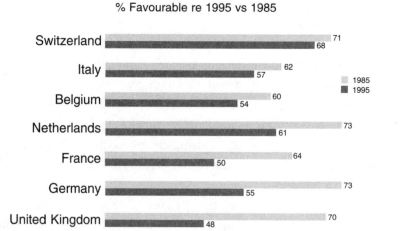

Figure 4: Relative employment security in different European countries. (Source: ISR[3])

worse than any of its competitors': from 70 per cent satisfaction levels in 1985 to 48 per cent by 1995 – at a time when UK Plc has been moving faster toward a contingent workforce than all of its European counterparts.

Will this trend toward stable insecurity, freelance working and virtual organizations continue? And more importantly, can organizations, virtual or otherwise, continue to demand commitment from employees they don't commit to? In comparative terms the UK economy has done remarkably well at the end of the 1990s, but the levels of job insecurity and dissatisfaction are fairly high. Developing and maintaining a 'feel-good' factor at work and in our economy generally is not just about bottom-line factors – such as higher salaries, a penny off income tax – or about increased profitability; it is or should be, in a civilized society, about quality of life issues as well, like hours of work, family time, manageable workloads, control over one's career and some sense of job security. As the social anthropologist Studs Terkel suggested,

> [work] is about a search for daily meaning as well as daily bread, for recognition as well as cash, for astonishment rather than torpor, in short, for a sort of life rather than a Monday through Friday sort of dying.[1]

As we approach the millennium, I hope employers will reflect on where they are going and what that might mean for employees and society in the future, and try to action their often espoused but rarely implemented credo 'our most valuable resource is our human resource'.

References

1 Terkel, S. (1972) *Working*, New York: Avon Books.
2 Cooper, C.L. (1996). 'Hot under the collar'. *The Times Higher Education Supplement*, June 21, p.15.
3 International Survey Research (1995). *Employee Satisfaction: Tracking European Trends*, London: ISR.
4 Walker, J. (1995) *The Cost of Communication Breakdown*, London: BT Forum.
5 DEMOS (1995) *Time Squeeze*, London: DEMOS.
6 Worrall, L. and Cooper, C.L. (1997) *IM–UMIST Quality of Working Life Survey*, London: Institute of Management.
7 Cooper, C.L. and Jackson, S. (1997) *Creating Tomorrow's Organizations: A Handbook for Future Research in Organizational Behavior*. Chichester and New York: John Wiley & Sons.

COMMUNICATIONS AND DISTANCE

The Deloitte & Touche Lecture

FRANCES CAIRNCROSS

Journalist, The Economist

The death of distance as a determinant of the cost of communications is going to be the single most important economic influence on society in the next quarter-century. Think of the effect the steamship had on the ability to carry goods from country to country. Think of the effect the car has had on our countryside, our cities and our lives. What we are seeing now is a fall in the price of transporting ideas and knowledge. This transport revolution makes it possible for new ideas to spread round the world and be adopted faster than has ever been the case.

With the computer there have been two particularly important developments. One is the extraordinary increase that has taken place year after year in the ratio of computing capacity to size and cost. A modern Nintendo game contains more computing capacity than the main processor on Apollo 13. The other huge change is the coming of a way to connect computers; they are now objects with which you communicate with the rest of the world through the Internet. These changes are fundamental to the revolution that is taking place because they have cut the cost of handling information and have increased the flexibility and the range of ways in which familiar tools such as the telephone can be used.

Another change which is even more important for the death of distance is the huge increase that has been taking place in the capacity to transmit information over long distances by satellite and undersea cable. This has already begun with the development of digital television which can squash on to the satellite transponder far more channels that it could before.

More information in less space

The most striking effect has been on the telephone and its network. Long-distance speaking ought to be the ideal use for the telephone but the fact that for most of its life this has been the most expensive and difficult thing to do has limited the telephone's usefulness. Now, a huge expansion in the amount of fibre-optic cable laid under the ocean can carry digital messages in enormous numbers. We are within sight of a time when we will be able to have the entire peak-hour telephone traffic of Europe carried on a single pair of fibres. On a well-used route like New York to London the cost of carrying a telephone call is already less than one-hundredth of a cent a minute. The additional cost of sending a call an extra mile is getting close to zero on the busiest long-distance routes.

Distance on some routes is as good as dead but it will take time before the underlying cost of transporting information round the world is fully reflected in retail prices. It will take quite a bit longer before the dramatic change in prices will be fully reflected in the way the world works. The four main areas of impact are: commerce, society, government and the nation state.

The impact on companies will be the first thing to become clear. Communicating is central to the way in which they do their business. They are more aware of costs. Above all, the transport revolution coincides with other big changes that are happening in the corporate world, such as globalization and the importance of ideas and services.

Marketing will be different. Electronic customers leave a data trail behind them; learning how best to use that information is going to be one of the biggest challenges facing corporate marketing departments. Advertising will become more personalized. There is already technology in the US which allows television commercials watched by an audience of several million to be tailored to individual viewers. You will see an advertisement that perhaps greets you by name and then tells you something you're likely to be more interested in than whatever is being shown to the house next door. Development of links between customers becomes a possibility because it is easier to match people with particular niche tastes. If you go to General Motors' Saturn page on the Internet you see a club for Saturn owners. All this offers a market of enthusiasts on whom you can test new products. It also creates a group of people who will be the first to complain and to swap complaints if something goes wrong.

Selling on the Internet
Commerce will be transformed. There are some high-profile electronic retailing companies selling, for example, books on the Internet, but by far the biggest commercial users at the moment and for the foreseeable future are businesses which are buying and selling products to each other. An Internet site run by General Electric puts up specifications of products the company wants to buy and invites bids from round the world. That one site currently does more business than all retailing put together. You can see why this should be. Company purchasing managers don't on the whole regard the process of shopping as a great deal of fun – but as the mother of two teenage girls I can tell you that Internet shopping will never replace the thrill of the chase up and down London's Bond Street sales!

A company's market is now potentially the whole world. There are still obstacles such as different standards, customs, languages and tastes but many companies now have their first possibility of looking for suppliers, distributors and customers in other parts of the world. In particular, there are new opportunities for small companies. The best-known Internet bookshop gets about 27 per cent of its orders from overseas.

There are other implications. When the Euro comes along and all continental companies are pricing their goods in a single currency, what are they going to put on their Internet site? Are they going to put the local price, the local Euro price, or a single price? That is going to be extremely important if the Euro lasts long enough for us to see the effects – but don't bet on it.

Distribution costs will be slashed for any product which can be delivered on-line. We therefore might expect to see a shift from spending on physical objects towards spending on objects and services that can be delivered on-line, because their relative cost will be reduced.

There will be richer communications with customers who might, for example, dial up on a Sunday night to check their bank balance by pressing a few buttons on their telephone or find out where their parcel has got to by looking up its reference number on the Internet. In all sorts of ways customers can be allowed to play a more active role in finding out what a company is doing and thus save it time and resources that are currently devoted to telling customers about it.

The revolution is going to create sharper margins, wider markets and better-informed customers. Already we are seeing the development of on-line auctions for items with a small market. If you have a quirky object which may have a large but scattered market, this may be the ideal way of reaching the customer and getting the right price.

Pygmies and giants

The other transformation that is going to occur in companies is in corporate structure, with more pygmies and more giants. The Internet reduces the barriers to entry for many businesses and offers an infinite number of niches; there is no space constraint as there is in the high street. We are already seeing the growth of many small companies – somebody with a bright idea and now an inexpensive way to market and deliver it, aiming at a tiny niche.

On the other hand, the industries which run these networks are showing a clear tendency towards greater concentration. The reason is simple: a network is more useful when there are lots of people on it. Network businesses tend to rely on standards because communication is easier if both parties speak the same language. This is true of machines as well as people. Once a standard catches on, the company running it is going to become extremely large.

Another change involves the three-shift company. If you can do a job on screen with a keyboard, there's no obvious reason why you can't do it anywhere in the world. Time zones will become more important as location becomes less important. A company in Bangalore specializes in repairing computer software for Californians. Before they go off for the night the Californians send their software to Bangalore where people repair it during their day and send it back in time for people waking up in California.

There is also the Hollywood effect. It used to be the case that Hollywood stars were salaried employees and paid not much more than other actors. Now the stars are freelance and earn more than the others. Companies may start to look like Hollywood today, where a loose assembly of specialists is brought together for one film. A corollary of this is that if the best employees become freelance stars they will have a clearer idea of what they are worth and will exact that price in the market.

Knowledge makes us rich
The second area is the impact on economies. The death of distance is a link between two key forces in the world economy: globalization and technological advance in information technology and communications. The basic building block of economic growth, the thing that makes us richer, is knowledge. The death of distance is going to make it possible for knowledge to spread faster so the world will grow richer, faster than it would have otherwise.

Output will become more intangible. There will be more marketing, design and intelligence; more of all the intangibles that are supposed to add value. There will be competition in new areas. Some of the fastest-growing services such as health, education and telecommunications have hardly been sold internationally up to now. Yet through communications it will be possible to sell, export and build world businesses in them. This will have all sorts of effects. It may mean that ordinary people will be able to afford things previously available only to the rich. A large American publishing group offered courses in biblical Greek for $34.95 and 2,000 people signed up.

A big redistribution of jobs both within and between countries will result but not necessarily an overall loss of jobs in any particular country. The businesses of amusement park rides and special effects in movies have benefited from the people who lost their jobs in aerospace and know a great deal about the sort of technology needed for theme park rides. The jobs that are going to grow fast will be in those sorts of industries. There are now more Americans making computers than making cars. Since 1990 the American film industry created more jobs than car manufacturing, pharmaceuticals and hotels combined. There is a relationship between countries that have invested in information technology and countries that have a good record on employment growth. There will be a widening of the gap between incomes within countries and a narrowing of the gap between incomes for doing certain jobs between countries. That will be driven largely by communications.

Where is the productivity?

Productivity is problematic. In spite of massive investment in IT, America is at the bottom of the league of big OECD countries in terms of productivity growth. Why hasn't information technology made economies more productive? There are three possible reasons. One is waste. When you had a typewriter on your desk you couldn't use it to play Minesweeper when you should have been writing your next article. Second, it takes time to learn how to get the best out of the new technology. The big gains in productivity from the use of electricity began to happen only when it had been in commercial use for more than 30 years. With computers, the really big change may turn out to be their linking rather than their invention. Third, the sort of improvements that you get as a result of communications are often qualitative and hard to measure. The biggest opportunities for improvements in productivity are in government and government services, but government is a slow adopter of new technologies.

Another big area of change is the impact on society and culture. Teleworking from home is not going to happen on a big scale but working from vehicles is growing fast. Using the car as an office is going to be important. There will also be a growth of the office in a box – the PC or similar equipment for use when travelling. The conventional office will still exist but there will be a change in its relationship with the home. People worry about the isolating effect of these changes, but they may provide an extension of social life. People who can't communicate now will able to. It will be easier to locate small groups with which people have something in common. There will be different sorts of communities from the ones we have at present.

English is the coming global tongue. It is to an astonishing degree the language of the Internet and it is spoken by more people as a second language than as a first language. There are fears small languages will be wiped out, but technology also offers the chance to cut the cost of making movies and local television programmes in minority languages, and there are many opportunities to develop cultural products for small linguistic groups.

Shifting the balance of power
Finally, government. Will we see the Big Brother scenario or a reduction in government power? The argument works both ways but the key evidence is that the nastiest governments have the worst communications. The death of distance will probably be a force for changing the balance of power between government and citizens.

It will be possible for people to vote directly on issues and for referendums to be held more frequently. Some people wonder whether there will be an armchair democracy where people press a button at home to say what they want to be done about a list of issues – BSE (bovine spongiform encephalopathy), widening the M25 or whatever. Yet since people prefer to have politicians operating on their behalf, there will be no radical change in the political process. More radical will be what happens to taxation. It will be easier for people to choose the country in which they work and therefore much harder to tax them. Better communications will create possibilities for small nations. When you don't have free trade it's important to have the largest possible national market but once you have free trade the world can be your market and the national market becomes less important.

There are some problems with the death of distance. Policing is probably the most difficult. This is a world where many kinds of transactions will cross borders, so it will be harder for national governments to enforce their will within their territory. Another policing problem is caused by the blurring of public and private spheres. At present there are different laws about what you can say in a private letter and what you can publish in a newspaper. That difference begins to blur when something that you say in an email may appear on a Web site and where it is harder to say what is and what is not in the public domain.

Pornography is shorthand for all the undesirable bits of information. The US starts from a constitutional defence of free speech but other countries have a more limited view. This has made the debate intractable. It would be intractable anyway because of the difficulties of policing borders. There will be screening techniques which to a large extent will keep out what you don't want to receive. The big problem will be to stop two willing participants from exchanging information that is, for example, libellous or racist, and to stop people saying things in this semi-public domain that they would not be allowed to say on television or in a newspaper.

There is the question of privacy. In a world where every electronic transaction leaves a trail of data it becomes harder to have complete privacy. Piracy is another problem area. Ideas are notoriously hard to protect. The difficulty will be to strike a balance between the need to ensure an adequate reward for innovators and the need to disseminate ideas that benefit a lot of people.

Is this revolution going to be good or bad? The car has been both a liberation and a scourge; the new technology revolution may turn out the same way. However, if it cuts the cost of transferring knowledge, the raw material of growth and prosperity, it must on balance be good.

CORPORATE CITIZENSHIP IN A GLOBAL AGE

DAVID LOGAN

Director, The Corporate Citizenship Company

My education in corporate citizenship took place largely in the United States of America, prior to going to work as Director of Special Programmes for Levi Strauss and Company in the United States. I had worked for the TUC in Britain, but when I got to America I was given a different brief. It was to look at how Levi's could be a good citizen in relation to its stakeholders. To understand the meaning of corporate citizenship today and to meet the challenge of managing it in the global age, it is important to understand the concept in the context of the historical perspective.

The historical context

In 1600 the East India Company was founded. It was the first 'modern' British multinational company and every question that can be raised about the social responsibility of today's companies was, in its day, raised about the East India Company and similar international enterprises.

At the height of its powers the East India Company contributed between 7 and 8 per cent of the British state's income; it conquered and ruled most of India until 1858, when the state stepped in and the company was wound up. This great transnational company helped to 'hook' Britain on tea. However, to pay the Chinese for tea, the company sold them opium because that was a product which the Chinese would buy for silver as counter-trade. Furthermore, tea was bitter and needed sweetening with sugar, and it was the European consumers' insatiable demand for sugar that was the great engine of the transatlantic slave trade.

The opium trade was bitterly criticized by both the Chinese government and British liberal campaigning groups. The East India Company was also heavily criticized for the fabulous wealth it created for its 'nabob' or 'fat cat' executives like Robert Clive. It was accused of overweening power in its relations with governments, bribery and 'human rights' abuses, which formed the background to the impeachment of Warren Hastings, Governor General of India.

The amazing success of *laissez-faire* capitalism at home and abroad, with its catalogue of social injustice and disruption, produced the hostile reaction of Marxism. Karl Marx wrote *Das Kapital* to help to destroy that system of international capitalism, and from the Russian Revolution in 1917 to the middle of the Thatcher–Reagan years dispossessed and industrial workers have retaliated against private business by seeking to destroy it or make it subordinate to the state. It is only in the past 10 years that Communism and Socialism – the chosen instruments of change of those hostile to private capital – have declined as major forces in global society.

The decline of state control

In the Soviet-style Communist state, the government owned everything and ran everything. However, apart from North Korea and Cuba, most countries today accept that in a modern society there ought to be a government sector, a for-profit business sector and, increasingly, a not-for-profit sector. The latter is small in terms of material resources but important to democracy; it is often where the spiritual and cultural values of a nation reside.

Margaret Thatcher and Ronald Reagan had a decisive influence in beginning to reverse a global culture of ever growing state power. Since the mid-1980s governments' share of gross domestic product (GDP) around the world has remained static or gone down. The

Swedish government, like the German one, has found that it cannot tax industry highly and expect to see a flow of inward investment. It has therefore given up trying to run major economic enterprises. The state has realized that it is a poor manager of productive resources in a world of global competition. Today, the state has to create an environment in which internationally mobile capital wants to invest and in which skilled workers and entrepreneurs want to live and work. This change in political culture has been driven by the forces of economic globalization.

In addition, governments also face a crisis in their own capacity to act effectively in the social arena. When Kennedy and Johnson were in power in the USA, 70 per cent of federal income was available for a vast range of 'Great Society' projects. By 2003 only 28 per cent of the US federal budget will be discretionary spending; the rest will go towards entitlements like pensions and Medicaid and on meeting debt service. Government no longer has the resources to cope with its role as 'provider' from the cradle to the grave. This is true not only of the wealthy countries but especially of poor ones. China has announced that it will not establish old-age pensions and has told people that they have to make their own provision; that is an immediate opportunity for commercial companies to sell pension plans. China is also cutting government jobs and abolishing housing subsidies.

However, the opening of world economies has also meant a massive opportunity for the expansion of global companies. China alone received $129 billion of inward investment in 1995. Mercedes-Benz has been reducing its labour force in Germany while opening a huge new factory in Alabama, the poorest state in the USA. It is taking agricultural labourers or people who have never worked at all, and within a few years is turning them into world-class car workers. That is the creative power of the multinationals and today developing regions receiving such inward investment welcome it. This is a far cry from the hostility to multi-nationals that typified the 1960s and 1970s.

The rise of global companies

Companies are perhaps the major agents of change in our global society. Each one has a distinctive mission, character and different values in investing, marketing, sourcing and other business decisions. Unfortunately, the economists have little to say about the behaviour of individual companies; they talk in terms of macro-economic trends while management scientists focus almost exclusively on trying to make companies more successful. Historians, for their part, tend to write from a nationalist perspective and few have analysed the development of great companies; which is a pity, because only 26 countries have a GDP larger than General Motors' annual revenues, and many are older globally and more influential than some nation states.

Denmark's $156 million makes it the twenty-sixth largest country in terms of GDP. General Motors, the largest industrial corporation, has annual revenues of $168 million. While these measures are not directly comparable, General Motors has 647,000 direct employees, each of whom supports at least another five jobs in the supply chain. If you give all of those employees and suppliers a spouse and two children, there are about 9 million people worldwide dependent on General Motors for their livelihood. The population of Denmark is 5.2 million. One might ask how long it will be before General Motors gets a seat at the United Nations.

In the Western world, while companies are big, there are other, larger, institutions in our society which keep them in check. In the US the top 10 companies are probably equivalent to 12 per cent of market capitalization, however in the Netherlands, the top 10 companies are equivalent to about 70 per cent of market capitalization. If Royal Dutch Shell alone (40 per cent of capitalization) decided to move its headquarters elsewhere to benefit from better tax treatment, it would have a profound impact on the Dutch economy. Large multinationals operating in small or poor countries can have immense economic and political influence. In developing countries, transnational and large indigenous companies are potentially very powerful; not least because they are often the main source of government tax revenues.

According to the UN there are 45,000 mainly publicly held transnationals in the world today with some 280,000 foreign affiliates. They are linked through their supply chain to millions of small, often family companies. It is a huge web of businesses equivalent to $7 trillion of trade per year. The corporate citizenship debate is about how these corporations behave economically, socially and ethically, as in the days of the East India Company – and, today, environmentally as well.

The rise of the not-for-profit sector

The main check on companies in the past was through the activities of political parties and labour unions; but these organizations have declined and different organizations are taking over. The Royal Society for the Protection of Birds (RSPB), for example, is a single pressure group trying to bring developers to task for the loss of the wetlands because migratory birds need them. It now has more members paying higher membership fees than all the traditional British political parties put together. That is the kind of profound change that has taken place in many societies around the world.

The not-for-profit non-governmental sector, as in the antislavery days, is a vital part of our global society. While it is starting from a low base of financial resources it is also rapidly growing on a worldwide basis. In the USA it is 6 per cent of GDP; in Italy it is 2 per cent; it is technically illegal in China, but it still exists. Not-for-profit organizations, like companies, are benefiting from the decline of state power. In Britain, for example, they have taken over large elements of public housing. In America they are major service organizations, with about 15 per cent of all employment in the charity sector, providing a wide range of social services.

The other role of the not-for-profit sector is to agitate. Business has learned that as it has gained more power the not-for-profit organizations are the ones that might call them to account, not national and local governments seeking inward investment at any price. Shell is talking to not-for-profit organizations in a way that it never did before, and Sainsbury's new supplier code has an endorsement from Oxfam. When MORI asked British people whom they trusted on environmental issues, the Worldwide Fund for Nature and Greenpeace got the highest ratings. Companies like BP and ICI are in the mid-rankings and government ministers came far below them. The not-for-profit sector has a moral authority that business must come to terms with.

Defining corporate citizenship

In law, corporations are, in many respects, treated similarly to private individuals. Like individual citizens they have rights and responsibilities and they are active in society in many ways, for example lobbying for their economic self-interest. Also, like individual citizens, companies have an interest in the political, legal, economic and cultural framework that supports their existence. To maintain the framework of society that supports them, companies need to play a wider role in society, as well as pursuing the maximization of their self-interest. A liberal, free-market and democratic society needs to be nurtured by both individual and corporate citizens if it is to survive, develop and deliver on its implied promise of freedom, stability and prosperity for all.

Good 'corporate citizenship' today is not just doing business and supporting charity, as in the American philanthropist, Andrew Carnegie's, time. During the nineteenth century he developed resources, created jobs, paid taxes and supported many ancillary companies. That was the positive impact of his business, but he quite happily cracked skulls, broke unions and pillaged the environment to get business done. He was one of the great industrial 'robber barons' like Rockefeller and Ford, who then later in life created huge philanthropic foundations named after themselves. This traditional model of good citizenship, with philanthropy divorced from mainstream business activity, is unacceptable today. It is behaviour in all areas of corporate life that defines a corporate citizen.

In the current model, corporate citizenship is seen as the totality of a company's impact on society at home and abroad through dealings with primary stakeholders such as employees, customers, investors and business partners. The community is just one stakeholder and not often the most important one. Leading British, US and other companies take their wider citizenship responsibilities seriously. Marks & Spencer and Diageo, for example, have a code of business conduct. They produce, in addition to their annual report, separate reports on what they are doing for the community, the environment and their employees. Behind these reports are detailed statements of performance of management control issues. As companies become global they take their values with them and increasingly report on them. One problem is that they produce gross numbers in their reports: how does someone in India understand what Diageo is all about in that particular country? Diageo is thus experimenting with systems of social impact analysis which disaggregate the corporate numbers and produce separate statements for the individual countries in which it operates.

When you ask leading companies such as these about their core stakeholder groups, you find they are close to having major social and ethical issues under control. If you ask the best of our leading companies about pay in developing countries, they will be able to tell you what the minimum wage is, the actual average, the industry average and what the company itself pays, which is usually ahead of the national average and often leads the industry. On the whole, the multinationals set standards for behaviour in employment in the developing world.

Environmental responsibility
What is new about corporate citizenship theory is the way in which the environment is now treated as another stakeholder; in part because the moral language used to judge human relationships is

now being applied to other species and the physical world. In addition, people are saying to companies: 'You're not just responsible for your immediate stakeholders, your direct employees, for example. What about your suppliers? What about their use of children who make your soccer balls?' A new challenge for those charged with corporate responsibility in the social arena.

The experience of those managers responsible for environmental matters offers much. They have followed their supplier chain from raw materials right through to retail and recycling. They can make sure raw materials are from sustainable resources, ensure that suppliers comply with company environmental codes and that distributors use catalytic converters on their vehicles.

Until today companies have not mapped the social exposures of major businesses along the product lifecycle – and we need to. When a company like Chevron starts to drill for oil in Papua New Guinea, it meets indigenous people who have never seen a bulldozer before. What is the social impact of that? What are the ethics of putting contracts out to garment manufacturers in countries where child labour is acceptable, though it is not acceptable to middle-class liberals in New York who buy the product? What are the social responsibility issues when companies make life-saving drugs which the vast majority of the world's people cannot afford to buy? Figure 5 shows in a simple form how this mapping can be done.

In order to stay in business and be profitable, companies have to distribute their energy in a way that focus relentlessly on the price and quality of their products and services. They need also to focus on customers and employees, make sure the suppliers work, and that the shareholders are happy. Companies have to please the regulators, take care of communities, and deal with environmental problems linked to the business. These issues form a bull's-eye at which companies must aim. Consequently, they are deeply resistant to diverting time and energy to address wider social issues and want to define boundaries of corporate responsibility as narrowly as possible. But suddenly one of these problems can pop up and de-stabilize a business. The fact that a company like Shell is the main source of tax income for a dictatorship which is putting down legit-imate opposition and hanging poets, is a difficult issue to handle for highly focused, performance-driven business people.

The East India Company had similar problems and one reason that it ended up in so many military adventures was that it had to take control of surrounding social and political instability in order to do business in an orderly social and political environment. The

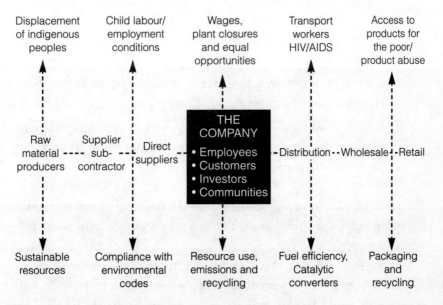

Figure 5: Environmental issues. The company in the economy: issues in the product lifecycle. (Source: The Corporate Citizenship Company)

problem for the company was that it ended up with such a swathe of administration to fund that it never made good profits again.

Companies are afraid of being drawn into an array of wider social issues and losing their focus on their core mission. They cannot do all that society might ask of them. They need the state and the not-for-profit sector to do their share, but companies have yet to work out how to operate effective partnerships with those organizations to create the climate for success, particularly in the developing world.

In order to resolve these conflicts, companies must take the time to map out their social responsibility 'exposures'; then decide why they should be involved in addressing them and how they are going to manage them.

The motives for corporate citizenship

Three basic motives underlie the corporate approach to good citizenship:

1   It can be good for business and can make a measurable contribution to the bottom line.

2   It is in a company's long-term self-interest to create the right social conditions in which to trade.

3   It is derived from a sense of moral and social responsibility which exists in many companies and leads them to seek to promote the public good.

Companies can be motivated by one or more of these at a time. Figure 6 opposite shows how they affect corporate action on citizenship issues.

Failure to address wider social issues may bring legislation: in the US there is pressure on financial service companies to provide new immigrants and minorities with access to credit. Banks had a poor record in this field. Democrats introduced the Community Reinvestment Act in the 1960s, which obliges all financial institutions to report annually on whether they give the poor of the US access to their socially vital products. Without a good rating they will not be allowed to expand or to close a branch down. That is the new role the state is coming to occupy in society, one of setting social and environmental targets for business, then monitoring and measuring its performance against them.

The people who manage community investment activity often relate most closely to the wider issues of social responsibility which

Motive	Characteristic Activity	Outcome for the Business
A direct contribution to the bottom line	Cause-related marketing and support for research in universities. Financial literacy programmes for potential consumers and investors.	Returns to the business are measurable in terms of increased sales, access to new ideas and qualified employees or product and brand awareness with potential customers.
Promoting the company's long-term self interest	Support for local anti-crime initiatives by retail businesses and work to improve education, training and the general environment.	The returns to the business are measurable, to some degree, by lower crime rates, better trained and more productive workers or good surroundings in which to do business
Promoting the public good	Corporate philanthropic donations and support for employee volunteering and giving. Disaster relief and support for employees in fulfilling public duties	Measurable benefits to the business are rarely sought but a reputation is established for being a 'caring' company amongst stakeholders and the public.

Figure 6: How motives affect corporate action on citizenship issues. (Source: Logan, Global Citizenship – Rationale and Strategies, *Hitachi Foundation, 1997.)*

business faces. It must be remembered that the community is a stakeholder in its own right, but it is also where other stakeholders, employees, investors and consumers live. Good community-affairs work need not be separated from the business: it can be an absolute asset to a company in understanding the wider context in which it has to operate; but good community relations are only a subset of a wider philosophy of good corporate citizenship.

In general, there are two broad and not mutually exclusive approaches to managing corporate citizenship issues. The first is pragmatic and *ad hoc*, while the second is values led. For example, in the environmental field there is a direct business benefit in cutting energy use: it helps profitability by reducing costs. Global warming is a wider issue. Many oil companies just deny its existence. A small minority of energy companies take another view. The values-led Amalgamated Energy Services (AES), an independent electricity-generating company in America, seeks to plant a tree to absorb every iota of carbon from their coal-fired power plant. It plants trees in the developing world and thus helps poor communities. AES addresses the issue even though it is not just that company's problem.

In respect of a social issue, the values-led company Body Shop has recognized that if the rain forest is going to survive, the people who live there need to have an income from it. It has set up a business to sell what these indigenous people produce. They don't have to move to the city and become part of our system if we take our system to them in a responsible way. These are small but significant changes in the breadth of company thinking about good citizenship.

There are those who argue that good citizenship gives you a competitive advantage in the marketplace. This can be true, but one has to be cautious. When you ask the British people if they want socially responsible capitalism, 95 per cent will say, 'Yes, I want my investments to benefit companies which are helping rather than harming the world population.' Yet the socially responsible investing funds account for £2.2 billion, or about 1.2 per cent of all mutual funds. We all know about ethical investment, but how many people have bought into it? There is a world of difference between expressing well-meaning opinions and moving to take action, even making sacrifices, to live up to them.

Whether values led, pragmatic or both, most companies should by now know that they cannot wait until they are hit by a crisis. However, few have the vision to commit management resources, time and effort to mapping and managing their complex relationship with the world. Companies need a significant internal capacity to monitor, measure and understand their global relationship with their stakeholders and to understand the wider social context in which their stakeholders live.

Unilever, a highly responsible company, views India as a market of 250 million people when selling soap and other personal hygiene products. It is forgotten that, in the Victorian era, getting the working class to buy and use soap was a major health issue and lives were saved by it. It was the private companies that provided the soap. Hand-washing remains critical for personal health; so we must ask: 'What about the other 800 million people in India? What do Unilever and other businesses owe to them? How does business include them in the benefits it brings?' This is a challenge to good citizenship and the potential for mutual benefits to business and society are real.

Society is willing to give business greater power on a worldwide basis but it wants to know what business is going to do with that power. If business does not sort out its own agenda in the next 15 to 20 years the state and the NGOs (non-government organizations) will write its agenda. It is time for each business to get its strategy for good corporate citizenship into place and then to move on to making it a reality in everyday business life.

Our global culture

For nearly 400 years there has been a low-intensity struggle between the state, activist citizens and the big company. Until 1917 the big companies pretty much had it their own way. Then people wanted to get their own back, and they did, with state control as the alternative. The situation has now switched back to private companies having a greatly enlarged role in our global culture. In the past 20 years we have transferred vast resources from the public sector to the private sector: the state and the NGOs are thus looking for companies to behave in a responsible manner. Worldwide, people want the benefits of free-market capitalism but don't want the social and environmental downsides. Companies can deliver more towards this goal than currently, and they may benefit handsomely in the process. However, they need to acknowledge this great change in global expectations and put real resources behind creating and implementing their own good citizenship strategy.

ETHICAL AUDITING: UNCOVERING THE SHADOW SIDE OF ORGANIZATIONS

Head of the UK Ethics Practice at PricewaterhouseCoopers
and
Former Director, ETHOS

The term business ethics is used here as a shorthand for workplace ethics – and the points which follow apply just as much to public sector and not-for-profit organizations as to businesses. There are as many definitions of business ethics as there are business ethicists. As a business person, rather than a philosopher or theologian, I am concerned that people at work should be able to practise the same kind of values that they want to practise in their private lives:

- trusting people around them;
- respecting their colleagues;
- feeling fairly treated;
- being open and honest in their dealings with others;
- expecting those other people to reciprocate.

What are business ethics?
Business ethics are a set of values practised by a company, or organization, which should meet all the legitimate expectations of its stakeholders; the values being acceptable not only to shareholders but also to employees, customers, suppliers and to the society in

which it operates. Obeying the law, complying with regulations of whatever kind, is taken for granted. Ethics concerns itself with the way people and organizations operate in the grey area above that baseline – where right and wrong are debatable and well-intentioned people may reasonably hold different opinions.

All organizations have a set of values but wide variations exist. One company might invest a great deal of time and resources in clarifying its values. They might start with a board retreat, then test out a draft with groups of staff, have the consensus confirmed by external stakeholders and finally undertake a full-scale training programme, to ensure that the values are not only understood but also put into practice on a daily basis.

Another company might just assume that the values held by the chairman are held by everyone – after all, he has been recruiting senior colleagues in his own image for as long as he can remember. The fact that the other 20 to 30,000 staff may not be practising Christians, have not gone to a school which taught blind obedience to authority, have not undergone military service and may be happy to pay higher taxes in return for better state education and an improved health service passes him by.

Conducting an audit need not involve imposing one's personal ethics. The aim is to audit the practice of an organization against its own declared values, to see whether it is meeting the legitimate expectations of all its stakeholders.

While the law acts as the baseline, all organizations have different sets of values. I look for a fundamental decision-making process and ask companies to consider the following questions:

- Have you taken into account the interests of everybody with a legitimate claim to be involved?

- Have you put forward all arguments for and against an action?

- Are your arguments of principle or consequence? (Arguments of principle in general carry more weight.)

Many companies have a code of conduct, but how do they know that staff actually live by that code, that it influences all their decisions on a day-to-day basis? The answer is that most of them have never checked. They assume that people act the way they should behave and then are startled, surprised, horror-struck even, when they don't. When I meet senior managers who are concerned with the ethics of people in his organization – and there are many thoughtful, caring managers out there wrestling with these issues – I ask, 'How do you measure the ethical performance of this company?' They invariably reply, 'That's a good question. How do you measure ethical performance?'

The ethical audit

The ethical audit is an attempt to measure ethical performance. It tests the coherence of that set of values. Ethical auditing evaluates the soundness, the internal and external consistency of the organization's values. The difference between ethical audits and social audits is as follows.

A number of companies have undertaken, or promised to undertake, social audits. Shell has recently faced a shareholder resolution which would have required it to undertake a social audit. The term 'social audit' has a longer history than ethical audit: it has been in use since the 1960s and examples can be found as early as the 1930s. The social audit measures the effects of an organization on society. It is primarily an external-facing process designed to enable the organization to account for its actions, though the less charitable view – and one reason companies may be resistant to it – is that it is designed to hold the company to account.

The ethical audit, however, is primarily a management information tool. I call it an 'audit' because my concept of the ethical audit is as a listening process. Auditing is listening, from the Latin *audire*, to hear. An ethical audit listens to the stakeholders - firstly, and most importantly, to the employees, whose voices are rarely heard. They have intimate knowledge of the day-to-day operations of the organization and know what is really going on; they know what the true values are and what behaviour really gets rewarded. This is what I mean when I refer to the 'shadow side' of an organization.

A 'shadow side' issue is one which affects the performance of the organization but which is never brought to the surface or confronted. A 'shadow side' issue is one that does not get discussed in any decision-making forum where something could be done about it. Not all 'shadow side' practices are bad – often they are employed to compensate for unnecessarily complex procedures or to sidestep ineffective managers. Yet, as Sir Adrian Cadbury has written, 'Openness and ethics go together. What is out in the open may not always be ethical but what is concealed is almost certain not to be.'[1]

Conducting an ethical audit

The purpose of an ethical audit is to inform senior management about ethical vulnerabilities. It will uncover potential ethical problem areas, the gap between official and actual company values, and ways in which organizational structure and processes prevent staff from doing the right thing. It can also be used, if management so chooses, to report on the ethical performance of the organization: in this case, the social effect, the effect on external stakeholders, will also be measured.

How does the ethical audit do this? It does it by asking the right questions and by listening carefully to the answers. It is a diagnostic process in the first instance. In future years, once a baseline has been established, it can become an accounting process, accounting for the progress over time. An initial ethical audit, however, can be treated either as a standalone exercise, which gives a snapshot of current shadow-side behaviour and consequent vulnerabilities, or as the first step in implementing an ethics process within the whole organization.

As a diagnostic tool, the process is straightforward. There are a number of different techniques – interviews, small group discussions and workshops. Questionnaires can be used as an introduction to the face-to-face meeting, designed to get people thinking about the issues and to check the demographics of the sample. I don't believe that you can carry out an effective ethical audit purely on a questionnaire or survey basis: designing written questions which will uncover the hidden side is extremely difficult and this is also a developmental process. Information gathered from one person or group needs to be checked out with others. The interviewer also needs to create a bond of trust so that the interviewees feel safe in answering honestly and openly. Sadly, in many organizations staff would not even trust the apparent anonymity of a questionnaire.

The benefits of ethical audits

What results might management expect? The result is that ethical vulnerabilities will be identified. These vulnerabilities may include anything from potential conflicts of interest and culture clashes (for example, overseas staff might think bribery is acceptable), to ways in which customers are being short-changed or suppliers forced to cut costs so dramatically that quality is compromised.

Opportunities for fraud are frequently uncovered through ethical auditing. Ways in which the structure and processes within the organization direct staff to behave unethically will be high-lighted. So much time and energy is wasted in the average company by staff fighting for their turf or protecting their backsides that removing the triggers which force this kind of behaviour can result in a dramatic increase in productivity.

Once staff feel safe and sure that what they say will not be traced back to them, they are so pleased to talk about these usually undis-cussable issues that the problem is stopping them talking. I'm constantly surprised how often, even today, managers simply do not listen to their staff, nor offer them opportunities to improve the way they work.

Although the aim is primarily diagnostic, the process of ethical auditing usually throws up a wealth of suggestions about ways to make positive changes. People do care about values: they do want to work in an environment which is open and fair and where they are respected for their contribution. They also want to belong and to be loyal. Openness is particularly important for company officials working overseas, who need to be able to alert headquarters to the ethical dilemmas they face, and receive advice and support, rather than being isolated as possible scapegoats.

Such a basic, diagnostic audit can identify many of the main ethical issues facing the organization in a surprisingly short time. Just one week of intensive conversations can provide enough input to give management the information to make real, productive changes or to put in place measures to protect the corporate reputation.

It may be some time yet before all organizations are prepared to commit themselves to a full, comprehensive, ethical and social audit. Such an audit would seek the views of all stakeholders, not just those of staff. When they eventually do, either from a belief in its cost-effectiveness or because regulation requires greater disclosure, shareholders and consumers alike will benefit immeasurably from the ability to compare companies fully before investing in them or buying from them. Society, too, will benefit: openness is the basis of public confidence in the corporate system. In the meantime, however, as an interim measure, wise managers will want to find out for themselves what ethical pitfalls they may be facing before someone else tells them about the problem. The ethical audit, the process outlined here, can help them to do just that.

Reference
1   Carmichael, S. (1995) *Business Ethics: The New Bottom Line*, London: DEMOS.

ETHICS IN POLICING

RICHARD WELLS

*Former Chief Constable of South Yorkshire,
Director, E-Quality Leadership*

The police service is for the most part task-focused. It is a
disciplined hierarchy and responds well to challenges which
can be met by structural change or by quantitative league
tables. In that sense, it is akin to the education and health services.

Far from undervaluing the importance of hierarchy, especially in
intervening promptly and effectively at times of crisis, I have
concerns that public sector services can be driven into too tight a
focus on task and structure to the detriment of their *raison d'être*. In
intervening in people's daily lives, police officers' actions impinge
on abstracts: people's liberty, sense of justice and sense of safety. Each
of these abstracts finds concrete definition in 'incidents' on the
streets, in homes and at workplaces.

Driven wrongly, the police service can focus too closely on the
detail of the 'incident', missing the broader canvas of the sometimes
complex interplay of freedom, justice and public safety. In the same
way, education and health services aim at potentially abstract
standards of learning and health yet attain those standards only
through the casework of people's lives.

In all three services, it will be possible to 'succeed' in the
casework sense – crimes detected, lessons delivered and beds filled
– but fail in the ethical sense. In the police service, this can bring
potential for great wrong and a consequent undermining of public
confidence.

Qualitative versus quantitative

The police have spent decades – not altogether completely or successfully – pulling themselves out of the mire of excessive focus on quantitative measures. League tables for stopping and searching suspects on the street, or for arrests and 'clear-ups' of crimes, have taken zealous officers into some pretty dark corners. At the softer end, it amounted to little more than fiddling figures to make them look 'better' – a pointless exercise when seen in the context of the large proportion of unreported crime or of the small number of cases resulting in final prosecution to conviction.

At the hard end, there are clearly documented cases of misguided officers fabricating evidence against people who were either innocent or, at best, guilty to a lesser criminal degree than the officers contrived to show them.

It is publicly and rightly acknowledged that the police service has led its own reform from within, whether spontaneously or as a result of external pressures of public and political interest. Most likely it was a combination of self-start and external push.

The most important aspect is police awareness of the need to change and police the effort put into it. The ground gained by those efforts is now under threat and a newly-won ethical dimension to policing is at risk of being displaced by the weight of quantitative assessment.

It will be the task of leaders of the service to hold the qualitative ground against the league-table monolith of Treasury thinking and practice. This does not mean casting aside any quantitative assessment as somehow inherently wicked or misleading. There is great value in the dictum, 'What gets measured gets done'. In a public service which, for too long in its past, failed to plan and to co-ordinate inputs with outputs, some disciplined measurement is both wise and appropriate.

Simply, quantity must not be allowed rebirth as the former shibboleth. This is different from recognizing that, along with qualitative assessment, some sensible, empirical measurement is good practice.

Migrating from a mechanical quantitative environment to an ethos in which quality is prized will take prolonged cultural change. The essence of that change will be from using people as a means to the achievement of a bottom line, to a position where people sustain achievement voluntarily because they are valued.

If leaders, especially in disciplined hierarchies, link fear and quantitative returns, they'll get impressive *figures* – don't ever doubt the human capacity to obey if backsides, jobs and mortgages are to be kept intact. However, the bosses responsible had best not ask – as with laws and sausages – how the figures are made.

If, on the other hand, leaders link trust and affection with qualitative assessment and some reasonable quantitative returns, they will get impressive *results*. This predicates a will to achieve through care for the people for whom, as leaders, we work.

Utilitarianism and altruism

Two principles inform the process of caring for the people within your command: the first is a utilitarian principle, heard most usually in the guise of: 'People are our most valuable asset'. People work better if they are happy and are more productive if they work better; win–win for the company, as morale up equals outputs up.

There is a second principle, less frequently advanced, which also informs the process: that is the altruistic principle. It is the personal responsibility of leaders to add to the quantum of happiness amongst those they lead. On bullet-torn battlefields, the increases may be small; in strife-torn industry, the capacity for increase may be greater. In each case, even small acts will be significant and cumulative.

At the heart of caring for people is recognition of each person's individuality: that he or she is to be valued. These words lend themselves readily to mission statements and what the facilitator for change in the South Yorkshire Police, Ronan Knox, calls the 'perspex tomb' – solemn exhortations and corporate promises encased in glass and as dead as the paper they are printed upon.

In reality, these sentiments *can* live and be practical in synergy between the utilitarian and the altruistic arguments.

Listening and hearing

There is probably no better way of valuing individuals than to listen to what they have to say and react constructively. In the Policy Review Committee (a decision-making body of some thirty senior ranks) there are regularly half a dozen observers from the 'sharp end' of policing. Actually, 'observers' is a misnomer because, at regular intervals, the process of discussion and decision-making is stopped to ask the observers what impact this or that action, if decided on, would have on front-line operations. The visitors contribute easily and effectively, sometimes shifting the direction of a decision.

The next to last item on each agenda is, 'How did we do today?' with members and observers alike providing direct feedback on the process and the tasks of the day. Observers will comment that this item seemed to take too long or that this part was given inadequate weight. Some express surprise that there is humour in the air and a genuine concern for their views; it is known that they go away and tell colleagues of the openness of the process – a simple indicator of success is that there is a waiting list to attend.

Similar value in listening comes through user-groups, members of which play an active part in assessing pieces of equipment or uniform which they select. Other examples lie in the quality groups, responsible for innovations in improved service, or in the consumer panels, who scrutinize draft official internal messages before they are issued to ensure hard-pressed operational staff will find them intelligible.

Close to the valuing of the individual in each of these cases is the aspect of transparency of intent: you are a team, you are a valued member of the team and your view counts in discussion. It is a matter of honesty, best viewed through openness of practice.

Honesty through transparency

This is the greatest cultural stride for a disciplined hierarchy to take: from a closed, fear-led and insurance-based ethos to one of openness, trust and innovation.

The fear generated by hierarchical strangleholds is not merely dysfunctional, resulting in suppression of creative talent, but can foster dishonesty. This can range from the inability of junior grades to express an opinion different from those senior to them, for fear that the fragile bloom of their career will fade, to the encouragement of cliques, favouritism, informants and the exercise of inequality. Worst examples of police corruption – 'firms within a firm' – have stemmed from just such a paralysing grip through the power of rank.

consensus

Opening up the hierarchy will bring equal and opposite forces of light into play. Role within the organization is stressed rather than rank: two superintendents meet with junior colleagues to discuss cross-border crime; they encourage a sergeant, because of her special skills and experience, to chair the meeting while they participate as members on an equal footing. First names are used in both directions, encouraging an adult–adult relationship in place of more traditional parent–child paradigms.

?

A chief superintendent, in early days of change, interrupts a more junior superintendent who is contributing to debate. The senior officer is stopped and his interruption criticized, allowing the junior officer to continue – the *role* of contributor takes ascendancy over the power of the interrupter's rank. These could be characterized as examples of *structural openness*.

Personal openness is important: the ability of individuals to feel able, in a safe learning environment, to express their feelings openly and with frankness. Whilst emergency services have to steel themselves to some awful jobs, suppressing their immediate nausea or anger or sorrow because they have a task to perform in the face of onlooking public expectations, they should not be put on an emotional pedestal. Ethically, people should be allowed a reasonable expression of their feelings without rebuke or ridicule. (Similarly, senior officers should feel able to admit that they don't have all the answers, that they would welcome advice before making the final decision for which they then accept responsibility.)

A final category might be defined as *administrative openness*. Members of the South Yorkshire Police were anxious about brown envelopes kept in their personal files. In these envelopes – marked ominously 'Not to be opened below the rank of Assistant Chief Constable' – were kept details of officers' personal careers. At an open meeting, the existence of the envelopes was challenged and the Senior Command Team made an on-the-spot policy pronouncement: nothing should be written about anyone which was not shown and copied to that individual. A logical development from this statement was that personal files should be opened up to the option of scrutiny by the subject of each file. The Senior Command Team held its breath, waiting for civil action from discoveries within the files. There was anger and disappointment but no civil actions. Scrutiny is now an accepted right. It has brought with it greater openness of reporting and appraisal, themselves vehicles for honesty. There are still brown envelopes but the contents of each (where it is necessary to keep confidential information about, for example, a medical condition) is known by, and copied to, the person subject of the file.

Differential grip

If all of this sounds a little goody-goody then let it be clear that it has tough edges. Openness and straight speaking, including the acceptance oneself of direct critical feedback, are powerful tools that require significant levels of courage and self-discipline. It is not a route for the faint-hearted.

If moral support is to be given to the overwhelming majority of good, hard-working and honest staff, then the few shirkers and rogues need grasping firmly where it hurts. The majority spot quickly the peer who is letting the side down and yet will not always be ready to blow the whistle. If they do, leaders must be prepared to act swiftly and fairly in support of those who have been brave enough to breach subtle aspects of peer-group loyalties in the greater ethical interests of the profession.

For the most part, this grip is the necessary exception rather than the rule. Fecklessness and misconduct are often tactical responses to poor motivation from leaders. It is a perfectly reasonable proposition to assume that mankind will try to work hard, do well and succeed rather than the opposite. In this lies the great truth of Blanchard and Johnson's neat proposition of 'catching people doing right'. So many structural hierarchies knock the motivational stuffing out of their staff by preying constantly on the small error in otherwise good work, so paralysing future initiative and creativity. The parallel dictum to 'what gets measured gets done' is 'what gets recognized gets done well'.

Quality begins at home
The final point is that all this must be harnessed, especially in a public service, to the needs of the customer or stakeholder. This is the ultimate selfless act of the service organization: to put the client's needs first. Most public services are poor at this aspect and spend a disproportionate amount of their time examining the fluff in their own administrative navel.

The act of public service is the synapse of the utilitarian and altruistic arguments. Quality begins at home within the organization. The way chief executives treat their immediate staff will ripple outwards through the concentric circles of the organization to front-line staff who will then be disposed to treat the customer in the same way.

If the chosen way is to value people, treat them with dignity, accord them their individuality, show them affection and make them an active part of the team, then that is the right thing to do, by any standards. Equally, they will more likely want to, and feel the need to, treat the client in a similar way. This is the utilitarian argument: treat people decently, then they will probably be more disposed to give decent service in return. However, to encourage the giving of decent, selfless service is itself an altruistic imperative. So treat people well because it is the higher human value; improve outputs by doing so, and the high ground and the bottom line converge.

TOMORROW'S COMPANY, TOMORROW'S PARTNERSHIP

SIR STUART HAMPSON

Chairman, John Lewis Partnership

It was at an RSA event in March 1994 that I first heard mention of 'inclusivity', the key concept of the Society's Inquiry into Tomorrow's Company[1] – the idea that a company will be more competitive and more profitable if it worries less about its financiers and more about its employees, its customers, its suppliers and the community in which it trades. In 1929 the Constitution of the John Lewis Partnership laid down its responsibility to take account of those same four constituencies – employees, customers, suppliers and the community at large – in the way its runs it business. I have become increasingly conscious that some of the things which we at John Lewis have taken for granted over many years have an importance for the competitiveness of British industry as a whole. They need to be brought into the open. Tomorrow's Company is about commerce sitting comfortably within society. The John Lewis Partnership provides an example of how this can be achieved.

The story of John Lewis

John Lewis himself was born in 1836, the son of a Somerset draper. He came to London and became a buyer for Peter Robinson's. The clothing trade in those days did not mean made-up clothes but the sale of fabrics, which at that time meant natural fibres, and particularly silk, rather than cotton, in high-quality business. In 1864 John Lewis struck out on his own and bought premises at 132 Oxford

Street. Far from being the retailing hub of London (then focused around St Paul's and the Tottenham Court Road), his shop had for neighbours a brushmaker and a dentist. He ignored the first three key principles of retailing – location, location, location; on his first day he took sixteen shillings and fourpence, and for six months he traded at a loss.

Then John Lewis had a breakthrough. He managed to buy a job lot of silk at a very good price. Instead of capturing a high profit by selling at the normal prices, he passed on the benefit of his keen purchasing to his customers – and from that point he never looked back. These are the nineteenth-century roots of the John Lewis Partnership's reputation for good value, encapsulated in our slogan 'never knowingly undersold'.

John Lewis became a highly successful Victorian businessman. The Long Silk Room in Oxford Street became famous for the breadth of its offer, including over a hundred different shades of a single type of silk, and in 1906 John Lewis purchased Peter Jones, walking over to Chelsea with the cash in his pocket. It cost him £22,500!

The concept of the partnership

Then there was one of those strange quirks of fate which changes everything. John Lewis had two sons, and one of them, with the somewhat unusual name of Spedan, was thrown from his horse and seriously injured. He was forced to convalesce for the best part of two years, and as time hung heavily on him he was able to reflect on his family business. In 1906 the 70-year-old John Lewis shared with his two sons, both barely out of school, a profit of £26,000, while the 300 staff took home wages totalling £16,000. Many well-to-do boys would bless their good fortune, but Spedan had an unease about such inequality. Looking across at what was happening in Russia, he could see the threat of Communism, and he didn't like what he saw. He therefore began to develop his ideas for a better form of capitalism.

Spedan Lewis looked at the fundamentals of what mattered in a company. Of course, money was important, but he could see that what made the difference in a business like shopkeeping was the employees. They were the ones who would deliver the service and win the customers. To be fair, enlightened shopowners (including John Lewis) looked after their staff, though in a paternalistic way. They provided accommodation for them to live above the shop or in nearby hostels; they equipped libraries with books carefully selected to improve the minds of their staff and to protect their morals; and they arranged services to keep their staff on the path of godliness. But when it came to real money, the staff did not figure. Spedan thought this was no way to build businesses for the long term. His father, however, had little time for Spedan's fanciful dreams, dismissing his son's ideas with the comment: 'Who would bear the carking cares of business for such a miserable remuneration as this would mean.' Here was a Victorian self-made man who believed that 'the carking [burdensome] cares of business' deserved the pleasures of wealth.

Nothing daunted, in 1914 Spedan won his father's permission to try out his ideas by running Peter Jones. He took over a loss-making business and promised the staff a share in profits if they could turn its fortunes round. And from that point on there was no looking back. He went further by telling the staff that they should decide the hours when the shop would be open, what holidays they should be allowed, and what should be done with profits.

The general view was that young Spedan Lewis was pursuing a ruinous path and creating a type of business that no one would want to manage, but in 1920 Peter Jones made a profit of £20,000, and staff were paid 'partnership benefit' equal to seven weeks' pay.

After his father's death in 1928, Spedan acquired control of the business as a whole. He set about applying the principles he had developed at Peter Jones and was now the sole proprietor of a growing business. He could have gone on enjoying the fruits of that ownership, but instead, in 1929, he transferred his shares in John

Lewis and Peter Jones to a Partnership Trust, so that from that date the business was genuinely owned 'by the staff for the staff' - or 'partners'.

Building on firm foundations

That is the folk history of the John Lewis Partnership and it is a tradition of which we are very proud. The key point, however, is that in 1997 it is still going strong. Spedan's idea wasn't a harebrained scheme doomed to failure. It wasn't like the worker co-operatives of the 1970s which blossomed and withered in the space of a few years – or even months.

In 1929 Spedan Lewis took care to make sure that his ideas on how business might be run would be sustained, that they would survive his own involvement, that they would not fail as a result of a company takeover, so we have a formal constitution which addresses precisely those four constituents at the heart of the *Tomorrow's Company Report:*[2]

- It commits the Partnership to offering customers the best value and the lowest prices; there's to be no backtracking on 'never knowingly undersold'.

- It acknowledges the need to treat suppliers with scrupulous fairness and to pay their accounts promptly (something which 68 years later is still enough to mark the Partnership as exceptional – indeed, failing to pay the bills is one justification for sacking the chairman, so I keep a close interest in that one!)

- It recognizes the importance of participation in community life through patronage of the arts, help towards charitable causes and interest in local affairs.

- Most exceptionally, it secures for all those who work in the Partnership the right to share in the responsibilities and prosperity of ownership. When we make a profit, settle any bills for interest on money we've borrowed, and put away

what we need to keep the business going in the future, all
the rest is distributed to our 36,000 Partners – not to
directors alone, but to everyone, in recognition that profits
are made by everyone playing their part not just by
directors setting the pace.

That's the way we run our 23 department stores, 117 Waitrose
supermarkets, the textile mills where we weave and print the
furnishing fabrics – which are a key part of the business's distinc-
tion – and 4,000 acres of glorious Hampshire countryside. It's a
varied demonstration of industrial democracy, and it works.

But what about tomorrow? Spedan Lewis died a disappointed
man because, having set out his idea of a new way forward, he was
not overwhelmed by the rush of others wanting to share his views
on an alternative to capitalism. Not until 1994, that is. Since the
Tomorrow's Company theme was launched by the RSA[1] a growing
number of companies have begun to recognize that the principle of
'inclusiveness' offers them the framework they need to gain and
sustain competitive edge. The Centre for Tomorrow's Company
(CTC) continues to attract companies wanting to develop in the
context of their own organizations the principles of the *Tomorrow's
Company* report and to share with other CTC member companies
the experiences which will allow them to move ahead faster.

In a book called *The Loyalty Effect*[2] Frederick Reichheld paints a
grim picture of the way much business is conducted today: 'US
corporations lose half their customers in five years, half their
employees in four years and half their investors in less than a year.'
He paints a picture of a future 'where business relationships are
opportunistic transactions between virtual strangers'. I find that an
unappealing prospect in terms of the kind of disfunctional
society it assumes. It is also a huge recipe for waste: every transaction
starts from scratch instead of being based on earlier shared experience
and understanding. Tomorrow's company, in contrast, assumes the
building of stronger and closer relationships which avoid waste.

Relationships with employees

The first key relationship is the relationship with employees. The John Lewis Partnership can offer a lead in terms of employee involvement, though some companies shy away from the lengths to which we go to share information, to allow Partners to discuss the profit and loss account of their branch, even to decide when our shops will be open. Five members of our main board are elected to represent our 36,000 partners. This is extreme, but if you can't trust your staff to know your figures, can you really trust them to deal with your customers properly?

Our structure does not stop us from succeeding in a fiercely competitive sector. With professionals like Fenwicks and M&S at our heels we have no scope for slackness. And our employees act as an accelerator and not a brake. Too many management textbooks have been written about the importance of shareholders, yet I have still to meet any employees who leap out of bed in the morning bursting to create value for the shareholders of their company. Successful businesses need to acknowledge and respond to human aspirations. I accept that there will always be some employees who work only for the pay packet, but what a narrow view of the purpose of work that offers, and how limited will be the output of anyone working on that basis.

Charles Handy, speaking to the RSA in 1996, referred to such workers as 'mercenaries', and pointed out that through history mercenaries have not proved the most reliable troops in battle. His alternative was a company run by 'citizens', who have rights in the company, who feel loyalty to its banner, who share in its successes.[4] At John Lewis we do our best to make sure our employees feel like 'citizens' and enjoy being 'owners'. We allow them to do exceptional things – sailing on five ocean-going yachts, fishing in one of the best trout streams in the world - not because they have personal wealth, but because they are members of a company which can do such things. As more companies resort to calling their employees 'human resources', we attach more importance to the difference of ours being 'Partners', and we value their loyalty to the business.

Citizens also have a right to be heard, even when their views are not always palatable. Our weekly magazine, *The Gazette*, has an anonymous correspondence page, where anyone can write in with their views on the way the business is run. Even though the correspondent opts for anonymity, the letter will be published with a reply from the appropriate director. This is a publication which is available to anyone. It is, however, a testimony of good faith. Any manager who is about to do something that he would find embarrassing if retold in the letters pages of *The Gazette* should not have been doing it anyway. It shows that we mean it when we say that the views of all our Partners need to be heard.

I do not claim that our arrangements for communication within our business are world-beating, but they do make common sense. A successful business needs to tap the ideas of every single member of its staff if it is to fulfil its potential, and every communication channel needs to be wide open. A representative of Boeing, the US aircraft manager, was quoted in the *Financial Times* as saying: 'I find most people have a lot of pride in what they do. If they're cynical it's because they tried a bunch of times to propose solutions, and nobody would ever listen.'[5]

Yet contrast this with the nervousness which is apparently felt about the introduction of Works Councils as part of the European Social Chapter. These are somehow seen as a threat to British industry. I regret that any company should be forced into communicating with its workforce, but I cannot understand how any company believes it can remain competitive if it cuts itself off from the driving force of its employees. Anti-European rhetoric seems to me an excuse for old-style adversarial management.

Relationships with customers
Secondly, let us look at relationships with customers. There's a lot of talk nowadays about customer 'loyalty', which really means putting a plastic card with a magnetic strip into the hands of as

many shoppers as possible so that you can make special offers available to them while you track their spending on a computer. John Lewis does not do this, but we are fully signed up to the principle of relying on the loyalty of our customers. It is our firm belief that, in business, loyalty cannot be bought by special offers. It has to be earned, and earned every single day.

On the Friday preceding the funeral of Diana, Princess of Wales, our Waitrose supermarkets were having difficulty coping with the unusual pattern of trade. Late in the day, a customer became irate when she found our shelves depleted in some areas, and she complained loudly to the manager about all the things she had been unable to buy. The manager listened and apologized. Then the following morning he came in first thing, went through the overnight deliveries to find all the items the customer had complained about not finding, got into his car and delivered them to the customer. No charge, with apologies for not getting it right first time. Doesn't that sound like a more compelling way of earning loyalty than any plastic card?

A few years ago, the BBC asked to do a 'fly on the wall' documentary on the John Lewis Partnership. We agreed and let them in. There were anxious moments during the filming, and the result was perhaps a little disappointing, but one customer said to camera: 'Do you remember when at garages someone would come out and fill your car with petrol. That's what shopping at John Lewis is like.' That quote made the programme worthwhile for me. She wasn't saying, I hope, that we were old-fashioned, but she recognized and valued personal service.

As technology increasingly allows dehumanized transactions (direct banking, direct insurance, mail order), the distinctiveness of personal service will increase. So also will the value of consistency. One of our competitors was having difficulty getting across to customers the value he felt his shops offered. One of his senior managers, who had been at university with me, was sent along to find out how John Lewis tackled this subject. I told him that our buyers set their prices at the lowest they thought necessary at least to match any competitor. He nodded. I said we then had people who checked every Argos catalogue, every Comet advert, every local newspaper to see that our prices stood up. I said we employed people whose sole job it was to trek up and down the high street to make sure there was nothing we had missed. He nodded. I said we paid our Partners a bonus of £2 for every item they picked up as slipping through all these nets. He nodded weakly. And finally, I said, we kept doing this for about 70 years! Reputations are not built overnight. They need nurturing. They need consistent conviction rather than pursuit of this year's fad.

I am convinced that the kind of behaviour I have described is the only way to build a business in the long term, to build relationships and to encourage mutual trust and respect. Yet there are so many pressures pulling in the opposite direction. Consumer organizations urge everyone to press harder for their rights, to write to the chairman, to complain more loudly. Legislation is based on the assumption that no one will give anything that they are not forced to give. These are signs of a failing society; tomorrow's company will act honourably without any of these compulsions.

Relationships with suppliers

The third constituent of inclusiveness identified in the *Tomorrow's Company* report[2] was suppliers. Here we are pushing against wide-open doors. Industry has largely recognized that the old-style adversarial relationships which characterized many business-to-business dealings are no way to secure efficiency. Any engineer can tell you that friction is the enemy of efficiency, and yet for years companies used to believe that driving a tough bargain from suppliers and screwing the last penny off the price was a sign of negotiating skill. Is it surprising that so many businesses ground to a halt?

Led by the Japanese, more and more companies have recognized the benefits of working together with suppliers towards the common aim of delivering a better product to the ultimate customer.

Relationships with the community

This leaves the question of the fourth aspect of inclusiveness, the relationship with the community at large. Of course, there is ample evidence of business recognizing the need to show respectable environmental credentials, and I am in no doubt that in coming years those commitments will become increasingly real; but the Tomorrow's Company Inquiry started from a concern about the 'licence to operate' of business, its reputation in society and the acceptability of its practices. In this respect the RSA and the Centre for Tomorrow's Company are in the process of changing the language of wealth creation.

During the Thatcher years wealth creation was justified by the 'trickle-down effect' – and it is difficult to argue against the principle that there are gains throughout society from the creation of prosperity. But the link between the City futures trader's Porsche and the lot of the Newcastle worker will always be far-stretched. Successful businesses don't just create wealth for a few so that from the profligacy of their spending a few crumbs fall to those less fortunate. Successful businesses create good jobs, they create fulfilling working conditions, they enable all employees to share a pride in achievement. Successful companies work with each other to build better products and to increase customer satisfaction.

The RSA's concern is to embolden enterprise, to increase the creativity in society and to ensure that manufacturing and commerce is respected. The ethical approach to business, as described in the *Tomorrow's Company* report[2], provides a basis for earning the respect that industry needs and outlines the path to competitive success – a way to enliven industry that is consistent with social cohesion.

A company with history has a great advantage as it wants to have a history in the future. Living up to inherited values and achievement is at least as strong a stimulus as the clean slate of the threatened takeover bid. The John Lewis Partnership will not be alone in applying 'the inclusive approach' as the RSA leads other companies down this route to competitive success and enables commerce to sit comfortably within society.

References

1 The RSA Tomorrow's Company Inquiry was set up by the RSA in 1993 to stimulate greater competitive performance by encouraging UK business leaders, and those who influence their decision-making, to re-examine the sources of sustainable business success. It is now run by the Centre for Tomorrow's Company (see page 77). For further information contact: CTC, 19 Buckingham Street, London WC2N 6EF; tel 0171-930 5150.

2 RSA (1995) *Tomorrow's Company,* Aldershot: Gower.

3 Reichheld, F. (1996) *The Loyalty Effect,* Boston, MA: Harvard Business School Press.

4 Handy, C. (1996) 'What's it all for? Reinventing capitalism for the next century', lecture delivered to the RSA on 13 November 1996 (see *RSA Journal,* December, 1996, pp 33–39).

5 *Financial Times,* 29 July 1996.

Tomorrow's Company –
A Journey of Discovery

Nick Obolensky

Chief Executive, Tomorrow's Company Enterprises Limited

The Tomorrow's Company journey began when, in 1993, the RSA launched the three-year Tomorrow's Company Inquiry, after Charles Handy's address to the RSA 'What is a company for?'[1] That culminated in the *Tomorrow's Company* report.[2] Out of that report was born the charity, the Centre for Tomorrow's Company, which works with the commercial subsidiary, Tomorrow's Company Enterprises, to encourage companies to adopt the inclusive approach.

The inclusive approach
In outline, the inclusive approach to achieving corporate success is about the company having a very clear sense of its purpose and its values. This isn't a purpose that is worked out by a few lucky directors who go off to a luxurious hotel for the weekend, with the result that, for some strange reason, the people who didn't go away with them do not share the same passion for the company's purpose. This is a purpose that is developed by the entire company in an inclusive way which embraces all its key internal and external relationships, and one that is shared. It is one on which a success model for that business is based, as the experience of Birmingham Midshires Building Society, our co-facilitators for the Pathfinder Project, demonstrates (see page 85).

Any success model for a business has to be managed on its key relationships. A business is not just about serving slavishly and exclusively the interests of the shareholders. It's about managing in harmony the other key relationships – the customers, the suppliers, the employees, and the wider community within which that business exists – which ensures that the shareholders get a very good return. We are too often constrained by 'triangular thinking': if you fill a triangle full of stakeholders, sooner or later one of them will come out on top. It's the shareholder or the customer or the company's people who are seen to be most important at the expense of the other interest groups. The challenge is to stop 'triangular' thinking and start 'circular' thinking: creating a dynamic like a constantly turning wheel. It is pointless arguing about which part of the wheel is touching the ground at a particular time. At a certain point it may make sense to concentrate on one particular area but it doesn't mean that is the priority for ever. The wheel goes on turning.

All of that demands the licence to operate that every business has. I ask many people if they can think of an example when someone destroyed the licence to operate in ten seconds. Gerald Ratner is often the person quoted, because with a few devastating words about his own company's products he demonstrated how fragile an organization's licence to operate can be in these complex times.

The Centre for Tomorrow's Company was set up to inspire and enable British business to compete with the best through adopting the inclusive approach. It has been supported by 20 founder member companies who share the vision, including the John Lewis Partnership (see page 65), Shell, Pertemps and Birmingham Midshires Building Society.

Changing attitudes
It is always difficult to measure the success of such a campaign and the extent to which the message has got through. We do know, however, that there has recently been a sea change in opinion

within corporate Britain. MORI [3] carried out a survey amongst the captains of industry which included a couple of questions measuring attitudes to the inclusive approach. We were delighted to find that over 70 per cent of the chief executives who were canvassed agreed with the statement that in order to serve share-holders better you have to focus on the interests of your employees, on your customers, on your suppliers – or partners, as we prefer to call them – and on the community. That 70 per cent is quite a different figure from the scant few per cent who held that view before the Tomorrow's Company Inquiry. The inquiry helped as an instrument for change. But some middle and junior managers claim that the message has yet to trickle through, so it is a glimmer of a change of attitude. Much still needs to be done.

Regaining competitiveness
In the age of Queen Victoria Britain not only ruled the waves; she also dominated global commerce with a brash confidence that was epitomized by the world's first luxury liner, the SS Great Britain. Isambard Kingdom Brunel built an iron-hulled ship of magnificent proportions, powered both by steam and sail, to keep himself ahead of the rest of the world. Today few British companies could claim, as Brunel could, that they are leading the rest of the world. Tomorrow's Company has sought to rediscover the commercial vigour of Victorian Britain.

The *Tomorrow's Company* report identified the root problem as being too much focus on shareholders' interests. The solution was a recognition of the rights of other stakeholders and interest not just in success for the next set of results, but success that could go on and on. The more the Tomorrow's Company think-tank of leading company managers and business academics looked at the problem, the more they felt that globalization, changes in technology and changes in organizations led to a view that unless one was taking every opportunity to beat the competition one was going to find it very difficult to sustain success. And taking every opportunity to sustain success means not being beholden solely to the shareholders.

The providers of capital, the City and the institutions are of course important to business, but what Tomorrow's Company is trying to do is to satisfy them better. Instead of only talking to them, you must talk to the other people who drive the success of a business: talk to your suppliers, really understand your customers, involve your employees, and be aware of the environment around you. If you do all of those things then the business is going to be so much stronger that the providers of capital are going to benefit.[4]

The Pathfinder Project

The question is how does this work out in the real world? The Tomorrow's Company Pathfinder Project aimed to focus on precisely this. Ten companies were chosen as Pathfinders, as a testing bed to see if the Tomorrow's Company approach really does work. They were a mixed group: Ernest Ireland, the construction company; the House of Clive Reflections hairdressing salons; Jungheinrich, a forklift truck sales and after-sales company; NatWest Insurance, brokers for the major insurers; NatWest Life & Investments; Osborne Clarke, one of the fastest-growing law companies (see page 95); Pertemps, from the employment industry, involved in both temporary and permanent employment as well as in outsourcing; Rolls-Royce Military Aero-Engines; Westec, who not only agreed to host and facilitate this process but were also willing to take the medicine and become one of the Pathfinders as well; and Wheale Thomas Hodgins, headhunters and recruitment specialists, a small company of eight or nine people.

Reflections, one of a chain of nineteen hairdressing salons owned and managed by entrepreneur Clive Barrett, found that one consequence of the Pathfinder Project was the appearance of one of London's top stylists in the chain's own training academy. Reflections Hairdressing believes that recent increases in turnover (up to 20 per cent in some areas) are due to the inclusive training and the approach learned from belonging to Tomorrow's Company. As Clive Barrett recounts:

> They are my people now, not workers. My clients are partici-pants. They set the agenda for the plan that I am now working towards to take my company forwards. I have now produced a five-year journey, not a destination but a journey, and when I get to the end of that journey there will be another five years, and so on. It's the most exciting thing that has happened to me from the moment I opened my own business 28 years ago.

The Pathfinder Project really was a journey of discovery.

Inclusiveness in practice

We asked ourselves how our mission 'to inspire and enable' could be achieved and what the inclusive approach meant in day-to-day practice. A few assumptions started surfacing. The first assumption was that it's not a question of some companies being inclusive and some not. It's more a question of where they are on the scale. At one end the scale is the paradigm we work towards: a totally inclusive company – even if we don't know quite what that looks like and even if we don't think there are any companies that are totally inclusive. At the other end of the scale is something close to a totally non-inclusive company. There aren't any organizations like that either, although some civil servants have been uncharitable enough to suggest that the Treasury may come close to it. (By definition a company or an organization that is totally non-inclusive cannot exist.) So the reality is that everybody is on this journey. Some people are moving forward, some people have actually stopped and there are some people who are moving back, but it's a continuum.

The second assumption was that, of 100 per cent of what a company needs to become more inclusive, 90 per cent is already in the company, so there is another 10 per cent which is needed from outside. Stretching this thinking further, we got together ten companies who were at different stages of the journey towards inclusiveness. One company's 10 per cent was likely to be different from another company's 10 per cent, which would probably be different from a third company's 10 per cent. The idea was that when all this was shaken out it covered that extra 10 per cent which each company needed to source from outside. It was an inclusive approach to adopting an inclusive approach.

The Pathfinder Project consisted of two complementary sides. On one side were the relationships: the customers, the employees, the partners or suppliers, the shareholders and the community. From these the companies themselves established areas that they wished to become more inclusive and, through 14 self-managed workshops, explored between themselves the areas in which they could share experience and seek improvement.

On the other side was what we called the glue, about vision, mission, goals, measurement, leadership, continuous improvement and all of those subjects that hold things together. These were covered in a joint workshop that Mike Jackson (see page 85) and I facilitated. There were also numerous internal workshops, the majority of which were run by the managers within those companies. The aim was for the companies to act as their own facilitators of this approach.

Two external workshops were also organized. One, exploring the supplier relationship, was a visit to Unipart, well-known for its work with suppliers. The second was a joint workshop hosted by the DTI and the British Quality Foundation to look at the interplay between the business excellence model as an excellent inclusive measurement process and the philosophy of Tomorrow's Company, and how they help each other.

The Pathfinder experiment was a blend of some familiar and some less familiar elements. With the benchmarking (see pages 96 to 97) came the value of not only sharing best practice but sharing the journey towards the inclusive approach, and the value of sharing one's problems even though the person alongside you doesn't necessarily have the solution.

We are now planning a series of Pathfinders across the country, as well as building on the current group in Bristol. As we develop the programme we learn the meaning of William Blake's words: 'I must create my own system, or be enslaved by another man's.'

References
1 Handy, C. 'What is a Company For?' lecture to the RSA, 5 December 1990.
2 RSA (1995) *Tomorrow's Company*, Aldershot: Gower.
3 MORI Captains of Industry Survey, Autumn 1996.
4 The three preceding paragraphs are based on the words of Paul Burden, business television presenter.

THE INCLUSIVE APPROACH –
KEY SUCCESS FACTORS

MIKE JACKSON

Chairman, Results Plus Ltd
and
Former Chief Executive, Birmingham Midshires Building Society

A few years ago the US CEO of the Year gave a talk to Birmingham Midshires Building Society. What he said provided a valuable illustration of the meaning of an inclusive approach (see also page 69). He explained how he had been running his business for 20 years, he was bored, he didn't know where his business was going and he was stuck. He was struggling to find out why he should actually stay in business at all. One day he happened to be sitting in a deckchair outside and saw a group of birds sitting in a bush. It reminded him of companies that he was working with or for: some of the birds were hanging on for grim death to some of the twigs, others were looking pretty comfortable, others were eyeing each other up and down, possibly contemplating a 'merger'. As he was looking at this bush he saw a skein of geese go overhead and he was struck by the idea that the birds sitting in the bush had been flying around aimlessly whereas the geese were organized into a shape and knew where they were going.

The aerodynamic approach
The first important point is that geese fly in V-shaped formations. Why? Because it streamlines their flow – so they clearly know

something the other birds don't know. Secondly, geese take turns at being the lead goose, very much like a self-managed team. They take turns because that way they don't tire themselves out so easily and each one has a role to play in getting all the geese to their destination. Thirdly, this observer discovered that, when geese fly, the lead goose takes all the strain while it is flying at the front and delivers 70 per cent more uplift, so the others can fly at less power to conserve energy.

The CEO was intrigued by this discovery and realized that this system must be better. He wanted his business to run in a way that could get 70 per cent more effort out of his people. That, to him, symbolized an inclusive approach and a great strategic success model. It certainly struck me and struck many of the people at Birmingham Midshires: the company now thinks in terms of trying to fly like a bunch of geese rather than sit around like a bunch of birds.

The four success factors

My role in the Tomorrow's Company Pathfinder Project (see pages 77 to 83) was to act as co-facilitator in getting the ten participating companies to think about their strategic success models. The key is to understand the difference between one strategic success model and another and to know which model is best for your business. Imagine a wheel with leadership at the hub and four points round the rim. These four points are labelled:

- strategy, direction and vision
- measures (goals)
- strategic core processes
- and culture.

The first challenge is to define the strategic direction for the business and determine how you are going to infuse the business with an inspiring vision, one which everybody can be involved in helping to build, so that you all know clearly where you are going. The geese know they are going somewhere in the winter to keep away from the weather and will fly back in the summer to exactly the same place. It is essential to have a vision for where you are trying to get to.

Secondly, there is no point having a vision unless you have measures and goals to judge whether you are getting there. What measures would you put in place to measure your vision and track how far you are along the journey? In the Pathfinder Project we shared that process, comparing ways in which we could produce a set of co-ordinated measures. You need more than one measure, more than solely shareholder value to determine whether you are achieving enough. You need a good measure of what you are achieving with your suppliers ('business partners' at Birmingham Midshires), of the effects of your leadership style, your relationships with your people, how they feel about you, how your shareholders are feeling, customer loyalty levels and what the community is saying. Not many measures, but very powerful ones.

Thirdly, which processes need to be put in place to match the strategic vision and the goals? It's no good having measures if there are no processes to measure the goals. If we don't know how we're going to organize ourselves to achieve our goals, like the V-shape of the geese, then we are going to fail.

Fourthly, the company culture is very important. Most organizations recognize that now. It can either kill you or be the glue that holds you together. Many companies don't know how to measure culture and wouldn't know how to change it for the better. The Pathfinder Project spent a great deal of time determining what sort of culture the ten organizations had, how we might change it and what we could do to understand what the gap is between the existing and the ideal culture.

Linking it all together
Returning to the model of the wheel, the links between the four points on the rim are:

- objectives

- systems

- behaviours

- and values.

The strategic direction and business goals can be held together only by the objectives. Similarly, there have to be systems in place to keep the processes and the goals synchronized so that the wheel will turn. The processes and the culture won't work unless the behaviours of the management team and all of the people facing the customers are aligned. The culture and the strategic direction won't work unless the customer values are clearly understood and the company is playing back the customer values to the customers.

Between the hub of the wheel and the four points on the rim are four spokes:

- figures

- words

- models

- pictures.

Many of the businesses that we worked with on the Pathfinder Project tended to use figures and words to communicate their processes, their systems and vision to the business. We all use words but we often don't use them correctly. We use too many words, or the wrong words or we don't use enough; our people are starved of information or we communicate unclearly, because we are not quite clear about what the four points on the rim of the wheel model look like. We explored ways to communicate better through words and figures and ways to create pictures and models of what a company is trying to do – like pictures of the V-formation geese model.

Changing corporate culture

The reaction to change in any company is always fear, uncertainty and doubt, so the Pathfinder Project devoted a good deal of time to talking about how the negative stresses of fear, uncertainty and doubt could be minimized and the positive stresses of challenge, achievement and excitement maximized.

When implementing change you have to work with people who don't change and who hold you back. 'Adventurers' comprise about 20 per cent of people in any business. They will pick up the ball and run with it; you probably won't be able to stop them. They are the ones you must nurture. Let them go, pick them up when they fall over, and keep going. You don't kick them in the teeth when they drop the ball, because if you do that nobody will move.

About 60 per cent of the people in a company are sitting there saying, 'I don't particularly want to change, but if I could see that it was going to work for me, I would.' They are the 'adopters'. They are waiting to see whether the adventurers are successful. If you get the adventurers moving in the right direction, another 60 per cent will move and you will have 80 per cent of your people going in the same direction.

That leaves the remaining 20 per cent, the abstainers. With 80 per cent of the company on board you have a situation in which the rest will be managed up or out, usually by the other 80 per cent, because they don't want them on board. Management doesn't have to start saying who should leave and who doesn't. By contrast, in some of the businesses where I have worked, the model is to shoot the adventurers and let the abstainers stay where they are.

Successful leadership

Leadership is the glue that holds the whole wheel together and the axle that makes it turn. There is no leadership model that works for everybody, and companies are likely to have different leadership styles because the leadership model drives your culture, your values and your strategy.

My leadership model has 10 points:

- Delighting stakeholders.

- Getting closer to stakeholders than competitors do – making them feel that they don't want to go anywhere else and encouraging them to become advocates for your company.

- Planning to do all jobs right first time. This means there is no delay, no error. Costs are reduced and customers get what they want.

- Agreeing accepted performance standards.

- Demanding continuous performance. This involves exclusiveness and is not a soft option. It doesn't mean, 'if it's inclusive I can do nothing.' It does mean that everybody has to be inclusive.

- Measuring performance. This means everybody's performance and the company's performance.

- Recognizing achievements. Just saying 'Thank you' costs nothing.

- Celebrating success. Much of this is just saying, 'That person over there has succeeded. We'd like you to do that, too, please.'

- Learning from experience. In my business we have post-implementation reviews on almost everything: 'Why did it go wrong? What do we do differently the next time?' You must keep learning from your mistakes.

- Creating possibilities and making quantum leaps.

Tools and techniques

For the Pathfinder Project we used many tools that most companies would never dream of using and we asked some of the teams to do things they had never done before, at least not since they were at school.

One useful process is looking at the political, economic, social and technological (PEST) factors that face companies in their business. A PEST analysis involves looking outside your world and starting to think about what might happen. Another is SWOT analysis, examining strengths and weaknesses, opportunities and threats, looking at how you can maximize the strengths and opportunities and by doing so minimize the weaknesses and the threats.

To explore, visualize and communicate a vision of where a company should be going and what it will look like when it gets there, you can use flip-charts, bits of newspapers, magazines and so on and stick them on the wall with your own photographs to create a picture of what you want out of your company tomorrow. This process generates incredible ideas and new visions of what people think, and gets everybody on the same wavelength. We tend to think only in words and figures and have somehow forgotten, as older people, how to communicate in pictures and models. Advertising companies use this method to generate the ideas you see in adverts on television, so why can't the rest of business? You can also use Post-it® notes to write up ideas and then sort them into what is most important.

New attitudes

There are a number of ways in which you can encourage your people to approach problems differently and adopt new attitudes. When somebody asks a question, it might not be the right question so he or she needs to think about what the big question is. If you have got a problem in the car park, is that the question or is the question really whether you have the right building or the right people in the building – and what is the bigger answer to the bigger question?

It is important to teach people that before they start doing any work they should ask what the purpose of the work is. One management team of mine saved 75 per cent of the time we used to waste facing each other across the table at meetings by making sure that everyone knew the purpose of what they were about to do, what process they were going to use and what the pay-off was. After that we knew what we went in to the meeting for, what we had to come out with, and how we were going to get there.

In any meeting I insisted firstly that people know what they are going to communicate when everyone walks out of the room. In my case at Birmingham Midshires there were 2,000 people outside knowing the meeting took place and wondering whether we were working on redundancy, when we were actually working on a growth plan. So after every meeting, we always asked what we were going to communicate when we got back and came out with a statement saying what happened. Team improvement is about inclusiveness, so, secondly, I insisted on establishing how we did in the meeting and what we should do to make the next meeting better.

Many businesses have difficulty drawing up a prioritized list of objectives in the right order. People argue about what is most important, but there is a way to cope with different attitudes. It involves developing a graph with 'important to me' on the vertical axis and 'important to the business' on the horizontal axis. Each axis is graded from low through medium to high. People use sticky dots to log their judgement and a cluster of dots denotes the top priorities, in the right order.

This is very inclusive because you can do it with 2,000 people, not just a handful. Birmingham Midshires tried to get all its people involved in the corporate plan. Once we had 500 people, 25 per cent of the company, involved and used this process to prioritize. What it helps to clarify is that you should concentrate on the top priorities, put the medium priorities on the back burner until you are ready to tackle them (but keep watching in case they change), and never start the low priorities unless you have done everything else. This tool has helped several of the Pathfinder companies to cut their costs and get more focused.

The journey towards excellence

As Nick Obolensky has said, creating the inclusive company is a journey not a destination (pages 77 to 83). Picture the solitary astronaut walking in space. He is fearful, uncertain and doubtful, wondering if there's anybody down there keeping him alive. But it's a great metaphor for the excitement, achievement and challenge. He is excited by the fact he is one of the few people who has ever walked in space, but at the same time he is fearful that the mission might fail. It's an inclusive activity because without the 2,000 people down below you couldn't get that sort of excellence. That's the sort of organization to which I aspire. Excellence can be achieved by the people who are doing the job at the back office as well as the front. The people who are gaining the fame are not necessarily the ones who made the mission possible.

The inclusive attitude is summed up as 'If it is to be, then it is up to me to spread the word about this excellent model for doing tomorrow's business in a tomorrow's company.' I recommend the inclusive approach without reservation.

Changing the Law – Tomorrow's Legal Partnership

Leslie Perrin

Managing Partner, Osborne Clarke, Solicitors

The firm Osborne Clarke is located on three sites: about 350 people in Bristol, about 100 in the City of London, and 20 in the Thames Valley. In the last few years we have doubled our fee income. This has challenged every system in our business and has brought us recognition as the third fastest-growing law firm in the country. Our aspiration is to be the dominant commercial law firm in the south of England and to be a national market leader in five areas: corporate finance, IT, telecoms, media and employment. Our values are fantastically simple and they are shared by every professional service firm because they are at the heart of professionalism. We want to look after our clients beautifully and, second only to that, to look after our people beautifully.

Facing up to change
The company is 250 years old. Longevity in a law firm is acceptable. People like to think that you are going to be there tomorrow and the fact that you were there 250 years ago is *prima facie* evidence. But how do you take a 250-year-old legal partnership and make it commit to change? It is tremendously difficult.

Lawyers live an exceptionally volatile life these days. When I heard about the inclusive approach, it struck me as a still point of values in a world that was exceptionally turbulent for us. We thought we were doing pretty well, and in a way we were, but lawyers are very quick to arrogance: they know the answer before they have heard the question. Any lawyer who thinks that he is good at looking after his clients and good at looking after his people should talk to Clive Barrett, the hairdresser on the Pathfinder Project, and they will find that their vanity is unjustified (see page 80).

Finding the right philosophy

Osborne Clarke wanted, in the midst of all this turbulent change, to find a business philosophy which addressed the values of the business. The Tomorrow's Company business philosophy helped us to do this and helped us to explain and articulate our aspirations for change. Our whole game is not about arriving at thousands of identical products at the end of the day. We are trying to harness the collective experience of the firm, which might reside in any corner of it, and to bring it to bear on *ad hoc* situations with teams forming just for that job and client needs being often very different and diverse. We are encouraging our people to get close to their clients, to dare to do new work, to press back the boundaries of their business.

We also have to match the values of our clients with the values of our business. Many of our clients, including NatWest Bank, have been with us for literally hundreds of years. We are in the business of loyalty. When our firm doubled in size over three years, our top 10 clients all stayed within the top 15. We understood the importance of the charm, judgement, personality, loyalty and commitment of our people. You cannot achieve this with a whip and a drum, so we thought we were doing the right things.

Cross-sectoral benchmarking

How do we learn in our business? What do we do to develop our knowledge? We felt that we had exhausted the potential within our own industry to benchmark our performance. In the legal sector there are quite sophisticated ways of doing this. We therefore decided to look at the standards of other sectors to see what they might mean to the business of being a lawyer.

Through the Tomorrow's Company Pathfinder Project (see pages 77 to 83) we were able to benefit from an exchange of ideas with a heterogeneous group that gave us a whole new range of insights. The scales fell from our eyes in all kinds of small ways. Amongst other things, we learned how we could adopt a more focused approach to our working partners, gain from staff satisfaction surveys – and how charity does not begin with C for chequebook.

Reviewing relationships

One constituency that we were really very challenged by was suppliers, or 'partners'. We were not treating suppliers in the way that we wanted to be treated by our clients as suppliers. As Nick Obolensky pointed out to us, if 30 per cent of your income goes in payments to non-wage and non-property suppliers, then 30 per cent of your value stream is in those people as well. We have now managed to make some very beneficial changes in that area simply by having the issue brought into the forefront of our activities.

The realization that 'our people are our community' was a dramatic realization for a firm like ours that was concerned about its community policy and had never recognized that it had a community policy already, and that its people were involved in that community. The only problem was to identify, articulate and support it.

The inclusive approach is a very important business philosophy. When the ground is heaving under your feet in a business and you wonder what the hell is going on, there is a profound conviction in your mind, which many share, that profit-driven enterprises fail. What is going wrong? The inclusive approach and the five key relationships on which it focuses are very sturdy braces to hold on to when you are trying to understand your business and trying to understand the changes and pressures to which it is subjected.

The future

We felt that there were things that we were good at but we weren't as good as we thought we were. We thought there were things that we were bad at but we didn't quite understand how bad we were at them. From this we have now managed to pull ourselves up with the help of our facilitators and fellow journeyers into an organization that is confident about its processes, proud of the things that we used to do well and proud of the fact that we now do them better. The journey is continuing. We now have meetings at which we decide what the valuable processes are that we can still share and how we can take them forward together.

When I think back to Jeremiah Osborne in 1748 who founded Osborne Clarke and William Shipley who founded the Royal Society of Arts in 1754, I wonder what they would have thought about all this. They would have thought that a vibrant economy is a very important part of a civilized society and that the values that the business community holds in that economy are of absolutely paramount importance.

We have tried to share the responsibility and the lessons that we have learned across the whole of our management spectrum, but finding time for new initiatives is always a massive problem in whatever business you are in, especially, perhaps, in the law, where there are a lot of people who just want to be left alone to get on with the law. There are many businesses who could find the nourishment that Osborne Clarke found through the Tomorrow's Company philosophy and an experience such as the Pathfinder Project.

The inclusive approach is a business idea whose time has come, because new values are taking over from, for want of a better label, Thatcherism. There is a more balanced view of what success amounts to now. The Tomorrow's Company ideal will thrive and

will go on to become one of the most important business philosophies of the end of the twentieth century.

The question is will I be able to be inclusive when my firm
ceases to grow so quickly? In a recession things start to turn down
and we have no jobs to spare: how will the inclusive approach help
us then? I believe it will but I believe it will be tough. It is always a
journey because life is a process and not a result. The inclusive
approach provides a set of tools that help you to respond to that
process, to understand it and to see what true value is.

THE LEADERSHIP OF
ORGANIZATIONS

PROFESSOR GARETH JONES

*BT Professor of Organisational Development,
Henley Management College*

W hy, in the closing years of the twentieth century, are we so obsessed with leadership? In all the organizations I work with, a key issue is: 'How can we develop more leaders?' The thousands of executives I have worked with always have two key questions: 'Teach me some finance so the finance department won't stitch me up' and 'How can I become a more effective leader?'

The philosophical background

Why are we obsessed with leadership? The answer to a question like that must, of course, be historical. We have to position our interest in leadership as a response to the failure of the rationalist revolution. In the nineteenth century, after the eighteenth-century Scottish Enlightenment, two other powerful beliefs were added to a belief in the power of reason: a belief in the inevitability of progress and a belief in the perfectibility of man.

One of the two intellectual giants of these philosophies is Karl Marx, who claimed to have discovered a rational order in human history. That's why he was such a fan of capitalism. Capitalism constitutes an enormous leap into the future compared with feudal society, and just as capitalism itself constitutes an improvement, Marx imagined some future order that would be an even greater improvement. He was probably a better analyst of capitalism than he was a predictor of the future.

The other giant, even more damaging to the pre-Enlightenment view, is Charles Darwin, because Charles Darwin, currently very fashionable, claimed to have discovered a rational order in the natural world. Butterflies are beautiful not because God is handy with a paintbrush but because they are rationally adapted to their environment.

The death of optimism

These notions of the power of reason, the inevitability of progress and the perfectibility of man come to constitute the nineteenth-century world view – a particularly Western view of leadership. Then the first cracks in this optimistic façade start to appear, as exemplified in the writings of two people.

The first is Sigmund Freud. At the very end of the nineteenth century Freud writes a few papers in which, portraying himself as a rationalist he nevertheless reminds us that human behaviour is not entirely rational, that lurking beneath the rational mind is a subconscious – in this early formulation motivated by the id. The id is like a volcano bubbling away beneath the surface, leaking into consciousness from time to time in the form of dream and fantasy. So there we are with this id bubbling away, primarily motivated by Eros, the life force.

Then, in the first decade of this century, in Western art and literature and music, there is a return to rather more spiritual concerns: What is man's true relationship to God? What is man's spiritual nature? People started asking very non-rationalist questions, such as 'how can we act truthfully?' They were the kinds of questions that would not have made much sense to Marx or Darwin.

As the twentieth century proper begins, we have much technological progress and then the two greatest nations in the world, Germany and the United Kingdom, go to war over 40 kilometres of mud in Belgium. Right up until the outbreak of the war no one believes this is possible, certainly not the Marxists and Social Democrats. Right up until the outbreak of the war they see it as inconceivable that the two greatest freely-organized working classes that the world has ever seen will fight an imperialist war. But along comes Kaiser Bill and says, 'Your country needs you.' And along comes Lord Kitchener and says, 'Your country needs you.' And off they go in their millions to be slaughtered on the wire of Ypres and the Somme, wiping out a generation of Frenchmen en passant. Survivors return to homes fit for heroes and we enter the wild and decadent 1920s: high growth rates, breakdown of traditional forms of social control, new sexual mores – exciting times.

The 1920s, however, end with the Great Crash. In the richest country in the world, the United States, a million people live on the railroads. If you read contemporary accounts of the Great Crash, it's described in pre-Enlightenment terms: as a plague, a visitation, a punishment for our moral excesses. We claim now that through the application of Keynesian economics we could have resisted the Great Crash. At the time no one understood it.

At this point, Freud writes a famous book, *Civilisation and its Discontents*, first published in 1930. It is a depressing read, because in it he says, 'I was wrong about the id. The id is not motivated solely by Eros, the life force. It is motivated equally by Thanatos, the death wish.' Those brought up in the Christian tradition will recognize that thought: it is the notion of original sin, the notion that there is something fundamentally wrong with the wiring, that we have a corrupt hard disk. The Victorians sometimes describe it as the worm in the bud.

Even the bleakest reading of Civilisation and its Discontents could not prepare for what would follow, for in 1933 the shadow of the swastika falls over much of Europe and the society that gave us Kant and Hegel and Mozart gives us crimes against humanity which we are still grappling to comprehend. After the first Allied troops reached the death camps in 1945 no one takes the notion of progress seriously again. That nineteenth-century optimism now seems a shallow promise. The road from Scottish rationalism in Edinburgh in the eighteenth century to Auschwitz in the twentieth century is a journey from enlightenment to despair.

The other writer who heralded the end of optimism, is my own intellectual guru, Max Weber. He was a German economist, philosopher, sociologist, historian and the foremost critic of Marx, whom he calls 'that clever German'. He said, 'Look, you clever German, why are you obsessed with capitalism? It's not the most important thing that's happening in the modern world. There are two important things. One is the rise of the modern nation state. But even more important than that is the domination of a particular way of thinking.'[1] He calls this 'technical rationality', where the logic of an action rests on the connection between means and ends, where the ends are given. It is a conception of rationality stripped of morality.

The power of bureaucracies

Max Weber believes that a particular organizational form embodies technical rationality: the bureaucracy. When we use the term 'bureaucracy' in modern everyday speech, we use it to mean that something is inefficient. For Max Weber what is truly frightening about bureaucracies is not their inefficiencies but their efficiencies, their ability to routinize things, to take individuals and strip them of their individuality, to process them. (This may explain why one of the largest office complexes in liberated Germany was the headquarters of the SS, organized on strictly bureaucratic lines, so prompting Eichmann's defence: 'I was simply a good bureaucrat.')

Weber believes that this way of thinking will come to dominate the whole world: 'mankind will be trapped in an iron cage of his own making from which he cannot escape'.[1] An iron cage dominated by logic and efficiency and bereft of morals and values. He calls it the disenchantment of the world, the removal of magic.

All this has a bearing on our attitude to leadership. The backdrop is that the late twentieth century is characterized by a moral vacuum, because we don't know what to believe in any more, hence the rapid growth of cult religions. Secondly, we are searching for something to stop bureaucracy in its tracks. We may speculate that eight of the ten most powerful economic institutions in the world are bureaucracies. So Weber was right: the world is dominated by bureaucratic organizations.

Interestingly, in British culture in particular, our heroes are anti-bureaucratic, whether it's Arthur Daley in *Minder*, Del Boy in *Only Fools and Horses* – 'no tax, no VAT' – the Good Soldier Svejk in Jaroslav Hasek's novel, or Yossarian in *Catch-22*. Yossarian wants to leave the mad bureaucracy of the US Air Force. Told that if he is sane enough to want to leave he is not mad enough to be allowed to leave, he is forced to feign madness and engage in ever-greater acts of insanity – further proof of his sanity.

What can stop bureaucracy? Charismatic leadership is Weber's answer, and it is at that point, in the 1920s, that our serious study of leadership begins.

The three schools of leadership

There have been three major schools of leadership study. The first is called trait theory. Like good scientists, the behavioural scientists tried to find effective leaders and look at what they had in common. There was an influential theory in the 1920s that effective leaders had wide-set eyes, and a powerful theory that correlated leadership ability with the gap between your nose and your upper lip. Trait theory broke down, however, when a very expensive American study concluded that (seriously): 'We have studied 400 effective leaders and we can conclude that they are either above average height or below.' One imagines a whole generation of American managers walking round either on tiptoe or bent double.

Then the behavioural scientists discover a new toy, the camera, so they start to film people and conclude that effective leaders have a distinctive style; they do things in a particular way. In the 1940s in

America this style is called the Human Relations Movement. It is open, pseudo-democratic, personal, affectionate almost. Thousands of mainly American managers are trained to adopt this style. There are even memory aids sold for managers so they can remember 'personal' things about their staff, but just as the style starts catching on, the world changes dramatically.

In the 1950s the world was on the edge of thermonuclear destruction and a whole new leadership style seemed appropriate: the Cold War warrior. Managers were buying rimless spectacles whether they needed them or not – and that was the end of style theory.

Then someone had the great idea of studying leadership instead of leaders – the relationship between the leaders and the led. It depends who you are trying to lead, which is why you have different leaders in a shipyard from a school, a hospital or an advertising agency.

That's clearly a great thought, but it's a complicated thought. First of all you have to ask, 'Who am I trying to lead?' Then, 'What are the critical parameters of the task?' Compare commissioning a power station for Asea Brown Boveri with selling more baked beans in Spain. They are tasks of completely different levels of complexity. Finally, of course, it is a question of situation, and a few historical blockbusters illustrate the point. Winston Churchill spent most of his life in the political wilderness, but under conditions of wartime became an inspiring leader.

The latest and best theory is therefore sometimes called situational leadership theory, which makes you work through that matrix: Who am I trying to lead? What are the most important characteristics of the task? And what are the characteristics of the situation which I can turn to my advantage? Jan Timmer, when he ran Philips, used to say that the Japanese had done more to change Philips than anyone else; that if they had not existed he would have had to invent them. He took the Japanese threat and made it a weapon for his own leadership.

Qualities of leaders

Out of that morass of theory come a number of conclusions that seem to be supported by the evidence, some of them from trait theory, some from style theory and some from situational leadership theory.

The first is that effective leaders are very good at collecting soft data. To use the psychological jargon, they have good social perceptual skills. They read the signs well; they have their ear to the ground. They know what is going on before someone tells them and they can tell the state of internal morale.

Secondly, effective leaders really care about the people they are leading. The trouble with that word 'care' in English is it sounds soft and wet. In fact it is a very hard word because really caring always involves personal risk. When you show that you really care, you reveal a little bit of your self-identity and you may be rejected. Leadership always involves personal risk. It means putting a bit of yourself on the line.

Thirdly, leaders have values and visions. Values need not involve motherhood statements. Greed is a perfectly respectable value and I know many organizations that are held together by it, mostly very successful. 'We believe in individual and corporate greed' is a powerful value statement. It doesn't have to be teamwork, quality and value for money. Vision means 'What are we going to do with this organization? Where are we taking it to? What will the snow-capped mountains look like when we get there?' We may never arrive, but we need to have some sense of what it would look like.

The important thing about both visions and values is that the visions must be communicated and the values must above all be practised. When a gap opens up between what leaders say and what they do, we have our worst ever problem: cynicism. And organizational cynicism is the curse of the modern age. I have stopped working with organizations where cynicism is rife. It's too difficult when people have spotted a gap between the rhetoric of the leadership and the reality of the practice. Whatever the visions are, whatever the values are, the most significant thing the leaders do is practise them.

It is important to understand that it is acceptable to be emotional about those things. There is a very interesting book called *Emotional Intelligence*,[2] which includes an interesting discussion of leadership and states: 'Leaders use their emotions to liberate the energy of others.' When you are in well-led organizations that is exactly what you observe – lots of high energy, lots of commitment to doing things really well, whether it's a pub, a bank branch, a hospital ward or a trading floor. As we struggle to come to terms with the notion that truly rational behaviour is emotional, and that truly rational behaviour comes from understanding and using our emotions, we will get a better grip on leadership.

A point derived from trait theory is that effective leaders tend to have high energy levels. They are people who persist, and when they get knocked back they come again. They have relentless energy. This is reflected in the slogan of probably the most successful change organization of the twentieth century, the African National Congress: 'The struggle continues. Victory is inevitable.' It's a wonderful slogan for any leader. You may not do 22 years on Robben Island but leaders get knocked back. Leaders depend on high energy to keep them going.

Doing it differently

The most important point, although it may seem cryptic, is that effective leaders are different. We don't follow people who are like us; we follow people who are different. In the Second World War the Eighth Army in North Africa was getting badly beaten. Then the War Office decided to do some organizational development, and they sent someone over and he said, 'Excuse me, who are we fighting?' 'Rommel.' 'Who are we fighting?' 'The Desert Fox.' 'Who are we fighting?' 'That old bastard Rommel.' 'And who's leading us?' 'Er, well last week it was a chap called Kevin. Can't remember much about him but he was at Sandhurst with me.'

The War Office decided to take a risk and sent out a maverick called Montgomery, who promoted himself on the plane over. This was not a man with much respect for bureaucratic rules. From an organizational point of view it was a complete turnaround, although strategically he was not an innovator in North Africa. From a psychological point of view he gave his group of people something to identify with. He wore a beret with two badges at the front, also illegal. It was not the first that he had tried. He was looking around for things that people could identify with, rather like Richard Branson's sweaters: using the difference. And he thought hard about how to communicate with his troops, deciding that the image of addressing them from the turret of a tank was perfect.

When I was a junior member of faculty at London Business School I was interviewing someone at 3i, which had just been founded as a fully fledged venture capitalist. After about 40 minutes an elderly gentleman appeared, wearing brown suede shoes and an old cardigan. I was rather upset abut being interrupted by someone who I assumed to be the caretaker. He walked in, picked up some papers from the desk and said, 'We've got 20 million in… . Get it out.' I thought, 'This is a funny bank, where the caretaker makes investment decisions.' It turned out to be the legendary Larry Tindale, the man described as having a brain the size of a house, who founded 3i to become probably the world's largest venture capitalist. He made his difference work for him.

One thinks of Sir John Harvey-Jones with the submariner's walk and the loud ties and long hair. Some people say that this is a bad example, because he used to run ICI and can do whatever he likes, but think about the young Harvey-Jones. Imagine him in his early thirties making his first presentation to the board. What are the pressures on you? How should you look? How should you behave? Like everyone else? The pressures are on you to conform, but leaders identify their differences and use them.

So when people come to me now and ask how they can develop their leadership skills. I say, 'Be yourself, more, with skill.'

References
1 Weber, M. *et al* (1993) *The Protestant Ethic and the Spirit of Capitalism*, London: Routledge.
2 Goleman, Daniel P. (1997) *Emotional Intelligence*, New York: Bantam Books.

LEADERSHIP THROUGH A SHARED VISION

HILARY CROPPER

Deputy Chairman and Chief Executive,
F.I. Group plc

L eadership is hard to define and even harder to embrace. Without it most endeavours are doomed to failure, yet with great leadership the seemingly impossible can be achieved.

Openness is the key to effective leadership. As chief executive of F.I. Group it is difficult to be anything other than open. When your employees own more than 40 per cent of the company's equity they clearly have a large influence on corporate decisions as well as the appointment of directors. But the question is how does the leader lead? Creating the vision involves three things:

- describing the objective
- understanding how to reach it
- and motivating people to follow.

It is not just blue sky visioning; it is the route march.

In the majority of cases the organization already exists when the leader arrives. In fact, the leader may emerge from within the ranks. Some organizations include thousands of people spread around the world. These organizations will already have their values, whether articulated or not, and their established ways of doing things, which are not always constructive or appropriate for the future. It is the role of the leader to challenge and to change the ambitions, the outlook, the pace and the behaviour.

The need for change

People might say, 'Why do things differently? Things are good here. Surely we shouldn't change for change's sake.' But the leader always sees the need for change. In these times of rapid development and global interaction, stability is an illusion. The organization is going either forwards or backwards; it is getting better or worse; it is gaining ground or losing it. It cannot stand still. If the person at the top does not create change, then by definition that person is not a leader.

Time and timing are critical factors. Most successful leaders remain in post for relatively long periods because change takes time. The larger the organization, the longer it will take to create the new mission and to ingrain the new culture. Leadership also demands a dedicated commitment to the achievement of described and predicted goals. The process begins with a wide-ranging debate which raises awareness of the issues and alerts people to the need for change and its essential character.

Sharing the vision

Initially it is important to have a team at the top whose members share the leader's vision and give support while the essential building blocks are put in place. After a period of consolidation, remaining dissenters will be quietly removed. (In the history of the organization this phase tends to be glossed over, but it invariably occurs.) If executed well, the change process will reach a point when the whole of the organization's structure, its philosophy, its values and operational systems are all supportive of achieving the goal in sight.

It is impossible to get close to this idealized state without the approval and active cooperation of people at every layer of the organization. What energizes them and galvanizes their actions is the perception of a kind of unifying purpose which is expressed as a set of shared beliefs and common objectives and the collective desire to win. This purpose must excite and stretch; it must be worth the sacrifice and risks involved. People believe in and follow the leader because he or she shows them the way forward and delivers the goods. Successes are vital. There will be numerous trials, so performance under pressure is crucial. In fact crises are often instrumental in confirming the leader's position.

The problem of power

Successful leadership inevitably leads to power. There is no shortage of examples which show how self-interest has taken over or mega egos have obstructed the way of progress. We have all seen cases in which people have clung to power long after disillusionment has set in, when the original entrepreneur suffers from risk aversion or when the innovator becomes the old guard. The stronger leaders are, the harder it is to budge them.

As we move into the twenty-first century perhaps we should put more emphasis on how to make leaders answerable to the people they lead. Perhaps we should stop talking about leadership and start researching what it takes to be good followers: how to balance the power, how to control the leader without stunting the energy and creativity they need to command the future.

In the F.I. Group we have established just such a system. Through employee share ownership we have created a formula which engages everyone in debating forward strategy, in participating in key decisions and in sharing the rewards they help to deliver. The City loves it. Contrary to popular opinion, institutional shareholders are entirely supportive, seeing employee share schemes as the insurance for their own returns. There can be no more demanding shareholders than your own employees. Share ownership means that employees have a long-term view in growing the equity of the company and are interested in making it a success. After all, theirs is a double stake.

TAKING PEOPLE WITH YOU – LEADERSHIP IN THE HEALTHCARE PROFESSION

HELEN TAYLOR THOMPSON, MBE

President, Mildmay Hospital

I do not believe that leaders can be made: they have to have a gene, however small, which can be cultivated and nurtured. Consider children in the nursery or primary school; one will lead and the others follow. I believe leaders are born, but many fall by the wayside through lack of guidance and support from their parents, teachers, or others who could have an influence on them.

When I was running laundry and dry cleaning businesses there were many gypsies, some of them illiterate, in my employment in one area. These staff had to be led quite differently from those in another area not far away. Leading people is rather like a game of chess with many different pieces all doing different things. Some go forward in a straight line, some jump about, some can go almost anywhere, but all have to be managed in order to reach the goal.

At one of the works I was managing during the 1960s no one belonged to a union. A union official arrived one day and asked to see the staff. Afterwards he said, 'It is quite unnecessary for anyone here to belong to our union. The place is so well run, everyone is happy and nobody grumbles. There is nothing we can do.'

In another area, at approximately the same time, the staff decided to strike for more money. I did what many couldn't do because of the numbers they employed: I saw each person individually, took them through the position we were in and explained the situation. The result was that we had no strike.

Rallying the troops

Mildmay Mission Hospital was originally founded as a small London district general hospital built in memory of the Victorian Christian, the Reverend William Pennefather, Vicar of St Jude's Church, Mildmay Park, Stoke Newington, who had sent his deaconesses out into the community to care for cholera sufferers. Later enlarged, the hospital was closed in 1982 but later reopened and became an AIDS hospice.

Napoleon, before going into battle, would go round talking to his men, giving them confidence and enthusiasm for the coming day. When I was rallying my troops at Mildmay Hospital for battle with the National Health Service I had very few supporters. In fact, just prior to the closure of Mildmay many people felt that the hospital had had its day and they were unwilling to get involved with a sinking ship. The few supporters that I did have were very committed to the cause of giving Mildmay back to its original owners and starting it up as a small community hospital. But the odds were against us and I was constantly having to rally them round me and, even when things looked pretty grim, keep their spirits up.

At the time when Mildmay had been reopened for just over a year the going was very tough, money was short and the authorities were doing all they could to close the hospital so that they could sell the property and get the capital. I was approached about whether I would consider taking a few AIDS patients. The idea was that we should mix one or two terminally ill AIDS sufferers with people from the community who were not terminally ill. This was not appropriate and would not have worked. AIDS at that time was thought by many to be extremely infectious and the patients untouchable.

However, I thought that it would be right for the hospital to care for people with AIDS. This meant getting not only the senior staff to agree but, more difficult, the whole board of governors. The local community had to be convinced that we were no threat to them. We had bottles thrown through ward windows and, regrettably, some of our supporters felt so strongly that AIDS was the result of evil that they believed we should have nothing to do with it. Looking back, this was possibly one of the biggest tests of my leadership.

I cannot explain fully how I did it, except that I never asked anyone to do something I would not do myself. I explained what was in my mind and I kept up morale. Mildmay became the first hospice in Europe for people with AIDS and it is now the largest.

Soon it became evident that whole families would be needing our care. I went to New York with the medical director and the chief executive, and came back convinced that we should build what is now the Family Care Centre, the first of its kind in Europe.

An international dimension
Very soon afterwards, when we were asked to go and start a centre in Uganda, I came up against a number of board members who couldn't accept the viability of going out to an African country and starting up a second front. Again I had to lead them forward. It isn't always easy and one can lose friends en route. The centre in Uganda opened officially in September 1998 with a prestigious conference for around 200 people from the whole of East Africa. Many other countries are now asking us to help teach them palliative care.

As a general rule those in the caring profession are not leaders and are certainly not entrepreneurs. No doubt this is why the NHS needs an overhaul. However, there are exceptions, and we have some at Mildmay. Becoming an AIDS hospice, teaching in many parts of the world and starting work in Uganda were major changes. Leaders need to be willing and able to change and persuade others of the need.

The world is made up of many different people with different talents. You should not attempt to be what you are not, but to be fulfilled in what you are fit to do. Being a leader brings responsibilities that must be faced if the leadership is to have lasting results. Sometimes it is easier not to be a leader, and many leaders fall by the wayside through lack of guidance and support.

CAN YOU TEACH LEADERSHIP?

LIEUTENANT-GENERAL J.F. DEVERELL, OBE

Deputy Commander-in-Chief, Land Command
and
Former Commandant, Royal Military Academy, Sandhurst

All of us have been in a position at some stage in our lives, whether at school, in the Services, on the sports field, in the workplace, or wherever, when others have attempted to focus our individual efforts for the benefit of the group. Many of us have at some stage been required to exercise our powers of leadership. So discussing leadership is rather akin to talking about food: everyone has eaten or cooked food and everyone has their own views about what constitutes good and bad food.

The question posed is: can leadership be taught? To put it another way: can you make successful leaders or are they born? Before we can answer the question, we need to examine what leaders are for and what leadership is. Successful leadership is immensely demanding, whether on the battlefield or in the workplace. Ultimately the leader has to get people to act in a selfless way when their instinct may be telling them to do the opposite and when failure to do so may result in catastrophe.

The complexity of the subject is demonstrated by this very believable story. There was an officer commanding a platoon of soldiers during the last war. Unfortunately, his soldiers felt that he was more predisposed than most other people to run away. But they liked him and supported him and made sure he did not. The

Commanding Officer, however, was uneasy and replaced the officer in question with another who was unquestionably brave. When the platoon was next involved in action, the new officer proved his bravery beyond all doubt, but his platoon refused to follow him, regarding his bravery as foolhardy and dangerous. This is an example of the illogical and irrational nature of leading and being led.

War is a singular experience and poses one of the greatest challenges to the robustness of the individual and the cohesion and effectiveness of an organization. There is little or no connection with the norms that determine our lives in peace. There are some who regard military leadership as relatively simple: all you have to do is to give people orders and they will obey because of the coercive nature of the military system. Experience tends to show that the commander who relies on coercion does not have a unit of any great cohesion or robustness.

What is a leader for?
Perhaps the first step in defining leadership is to ask what the leader is there for. At its simplest, a leader is there to ensure that a given task is successfully carried out by a group. The leader must understand what the task is, must have the requisite knowledge to use the resources available to complete it successfully, and must be acknowledged as the leader by the group. Thus leadership is essentially task-oriented. If someone is given a boring or disagreeable task it is very difficult to generate enthusiasm, however charismatic the leader is. It is easier with an interesting task, even one that is difficult or dangerous. The task has an effect on enthusiasm and may be part of the engine that drives the group.

It is too easy, however, to see leadership only in these terms and to become fixated by systems and structures. Leading is more than just doing; it is also about being. It is about what you are and what values you represent. Groups require a sense of purpose and the cohesion that this brings.

As cadets at Sandhurst in the mid 1960s, we were brought up on

John Adair's three-circle model of leadership in which three over-lapping circles represent the task, the team and the individual. The three elements are interdependent and must be kept in balance. The model also makes it clear that individuals must be prepared to give up some of their individual freedom of action for the good of the group.[1] The level to which this will be required depends on the situation, but the requirement for individuals to subordinate them-selves to the group, and to the task, tends to run counter to a 'me-oriented' society in which rights grow more in importance than responsibilities.

'Doing' and 'being'

The relationship between doing and being is reflected in British military doctrine. The key components of fighting power are the physical (manpower, resources), the conceptual or doing (doctrine, decision-making) and the moral or being (morale, mental robust-ness, professional ethics). Marshal Saxe, one of Napoleon's marshals said: 'There is nothing more important in war than the human heart. In a knowledge of the heart must be sought the secrets of the success and failure of armies.'[2]

The moral component of what the leader has to be is important in an army in a way that perhaps it is not in civilian life, though some might feel that in recent times there has been too much emphasis on what leaders have to do rather than what they have to be. For leaders to lead effectively in a direction that a democratic society would wish, there has to be an acceptance of moral values and humanity. Once we start to delve into being rather than doing, we are confronted by intangible and perhaps unfashionable concepts of duty, service, example, motivation and so on. These virtues lie at the heart of effective leadership and it is the actions that flow from them that demonstrate what the leader is as much as what the leader knows.

In his book, *The Anatomy of Courage*, Lord Moran refers to 'the electrifying effect of an act of coolness and courage' on those who see it.³ In his television series on heroes Brian Walden referred to the stirring impact of Churchill's wartime speeches upon him. At its most extreme we are talking about something that is inspirational and that plays on people's emotions.

Personal qualilties

If military leadership has ultimately to be inspiring, or even heroic, then personal qualities lie at the very heart of it, supported by structures and systems. It is for this reason that the British Army, like most others, concentrates on the study of leadership through the study of personal qualities. However, perhaps surprisingly, if you were to visit the military training establishments of different nations you would find little agreement as to what those qualities might be, but you will seldom find a list that does not contain, amongst others, courage, willpower, initiative and integrity – not necessarily in that order. These qualities tend to be general human qualities. I would hope that bank managers, doctors, and advertising executives all have them, too. There is nothing specifically military about them and it would be difficult to identify a personal quality required only by the military.

From Agincourt to IT

Leadership is only one part of command, however. Only so much can be achieved by exhortation or heroic example. Decision-making processes and the hierarchies of command and control provide the systems and structures that enable the commander to exercise his command. The command and control systems exercised by Wellington on the field of Waterloo in 1815 were little different from those used at Agincourt in 1415. The changes since, caused largely by technological and social development, have been immense, but they are more about what commanders have to do, and the way that they have to do it, than what they have to be.

Wellington practised heroic leadership because it was the only way that he could see the battlefield and thus exercise effective command and control. To do this, he had to put himself at risk of death or injury. Soldiers therefore saw him braving the same conditions that they were experiencing, which was one clue to his great popularity. Today the enormous power of modern surveillance and information systems tends to keep the commander safe, warm and well fed in the command bunker. To leave it is to reduce your vision of the battle because you are limiting the information and advice available to you. The heroic style is increasingly the preserve of junior officers and NCOs, and this raises some interesting leadership issues for more senior commanders. That aside, the essential personal qualities required of a commander seem to have stood the test of time and so are unlikely to change in the future.

Example and persuasion
For me, however, leadership is not best defined by lists of discrete and abstract qualities. There is more to it than that. One of the most helpful definitions of leadership was by Field Marshal Slim, who said that 'leadership is a mixture of example, persuasion and compulsion . . . In fact it is just plain you'.[4] The beauty of this definition is that it implies that leadership is a coat of many colours, with styles that can be mixed to suit the people and the situation. It also raises the issue of compulsion. I suspect Slim consciously puts compulsion last and example first because it was his view that a good soldier did things because he knew them to be right rather than because he had to. Thus compulsion, though an influential element in military leadership, is not of overriding importance.

One of the most famous Socratic paradoxes concerned the relationship between goodness and knowledge. Socrates accepted that knowledge could be taught. He also agreed that we could all point to examples of good behaviour, but when it came to defining it, it proved remarkably difficult. If we cannot define goodness – and Socrates never managed to – how can we teach it? In the dialogue in which Socrates discussed this matter, Protagoras presents his belief that goodness, which he defined as respect for others and a sense of justice, is possessed by all men in varying degrees because it is essential to human survival. He believed that goodness was taught, that fathers taught their sons how to conduct themselves, mostly by their own example. Because he believed that goodness could be taught, he also believed that individual goodness could be improved by tuition.

If we relate this to leadership, we can see that the knowledge to which Socrates and Protagoras refer could be seen as the mechanical processes – the structures, systems and procedures. Goodness is more akin to the personal qualities of courage, integrity and so on. We know that we can teach the mechanics, but can we teach the personal qualities? If you agree with Protagoras' view that everyone possesses some level of innate goodness and is capable of improvement, then assuming a person has some innate qualities of leadership, we should be able to teach leadership.

Does that mean that leaders are made, not born? Not quite. The leader must possess something more than charisma. Knowledge is a crucial element in the effectiveness of a leader. It may sometimes be simple, like being the one who can read the map or speak the language, but it is normally more complex. The military leader must understand, among other things, the structure in which he will fight, the command and control systems, the equipment and the reason why he is fighting. This part is easy to teach because it is essentially factual. At Sandhurst we could probably teach the officer cadet what an officer has to know in five months or so. Teaching what the officer has to be takes a lot longer, is more difficult and does not stop when the officer is commissioned. To teach a person to be courageous, to develop their determination, willpower and integrity and to use their initiative represents a substantial challenge to the trainer.

Selection systems

In the army we know from experience that there are those whose levels of innate ability are such that they will never, however much they are trained, reach the standards that will fit them for leadership in the more demanding areas. Therefore the recognition of potential is a key factor. If we are to produce leaders of ability, we need an effective selection system and it will be primarily focused on the personal qualities of the candidate. Manchester United would never consider allowing a football apprentice to join the staff if they did not think he had the innate ability to make the grade at the highest level.

Assuming that we have an effective selection system, how do we approach the teaching of leadership? A popular approach in the past, which still has its uses, has been to study how the great leaders of history have done it. But there are disadvantages in this method. Sometimes the qualities that made a very senior commander great can be a positive vice in someone more junior. Basil Liddell Hart said of Montgomery: 'as a young officer he did not show the natural signs of leadership, or the knack of handling men. When he was finally given command of a battalion …. He brought it to the verge of mutiny by misjudged handling.'[5] If case histories are of only limited value, what else? We can return to Slim's definition of leadership for an answer, since he not only tells us what leadership is, but also gives us a clue as to how we might teach it: leadership is a mixture of example and persuasion.

It may seem strange that persuasion is part of this, but while it is true that most soldiers who wish to join the Army do so because they aspire to become part of a structured and value-based society, they also come with some baggage from their previous lives. They are not necessarily as amenable to the demands and requirements of military life as some of their quite recent forebears. At an early stage we have to start convincing them of the value of personal qualities and the practical implications of, for example, integrity, in their lives: how one's personal conduct is important if one is to embrace the military ethos fully. Some soldiers may question whether private life influences military employability. Does the Army have a right, or a need, to uphold standards long since cast aside by others? Many potentially good soldiers may not accept the answers at face value. Thus the art of persuasion is a very important one.

Military ethos can be effectively taught only by example, by a process of osmosis. The ethos may be codified so that we know what it is, but unless the organization understands and exemplifies its ethos by the standards of those who are within it, the ethos will not be passed on. In fact, if it is not openly demonstrated as a matter of course, then in practice it doesn't exist, even if it is written down.

Learning by doing

It is not enough to be immersed in the right kind of environment, however. It is essential to practise leadership skills, so that leaders are given the opportunity to learn by experience, to gain confidence in their ability to understand and implement the basics. Equally, it is important that they learn that practical training in difficult and arduous conditions gives them the confidence that they can cope with future stress and control their fear. The training must also encourage them to develop their willpower and initiative. Testing not only gives the trainer the opportunity to assess and advise, but gives the trainee leaders the confidence that they can successfully meet the challenges ahead. Testing is carried out by putting them in positions of responsibility with sufficient room for manoeuvre, so that they are forced to make decisions which will determine the success or otherwise of the exercise or project. It is paradoxical that teaching some rather abstract ideas is best achieved by a practical rather than theoretical process.

The qualities I have been discussing apply as much to civilian life as to the armed forces, but there are some limitations. There have been plenty of examples of leadership courses that put civilians in adverse conditions so that they find their strengths and weaknesses. These courses encourage self-knowledge and self-development. Whether they develop leadership that is readily transferable is debatable. The structures that we use in military training are readily applicable to what soldiers have to do when they get to their regiment. This is not necessarily so for a banker or an advertising executive. It is for others to decide the value of such training. What is clear is that if we are to develop the personal qualities of people, it is effectively done by the practical application of those qualities in testing conditions.

There is an additional problem. If the values being projected by the training organization are not the same as those that underpin the institution within which the trainees operate, there may be some discontinuity when they return to their place of work. It is like teaching an offender in prison to be honest, when he finds that that the only way he can survive when he is released is by being dishonest.

We might be able to teach leadership, but can we make great leaders? Great leaders have normally been full of contradictions and one only has to list a series of great men to see that almost all were flawed in some way or another. Art teachers can teach students to draw, but can they make them great artists? I think not – there is something in the great artist that comes from within, and that is the difference between plain excellence and greatness.

There is also the question of whether we need to train people to be led. People sometimes say that they are not prepared to respect a person unless that person has demonstrated that he or she is worthy of respect. I have always thought that to be a depressingly negative attitude. There exists in many institutions a capital sum of goodwill towards leaders, generated by their predecessors. The new and inexperienced leader will use up some of this captial early on as he or she makes mistakes, but must then repay the balance whilst gaining experience and confidence. If not, leadership is doubly difficult.

In the Army we spend a good deal of time training young recruits in the part they are expected to play in the team and teaching them what they should expect of those who are to lead them – we train them how to be led. This process of establishing an appropriate and proper respect for authority is a difficult area and is as much the province of parents as of schools and other teaching organizations, but it is not something we can disregard.

The Royal Military Academy motto is 'Serve to Lead'. Like most mottoes it can be read in several different ways. It can mean that those who lead are servants of those whom they lead. It can also mean that in order to lead one has to learn how to serve. Neither definition is mutually exclusive, and officer cadets at the RMA spend time learning what it is like to be under command at the lowest level.

In conclusion, there are some people who are born leaders or at least whose leadership skills are acquired at an early age by whatever means. It is innate qualities that can make a leader great, but no leader can be effective without being trained in both the mechanistic processes and the moral dimension – the doing and the being. This presents both the trainer and the trainee with the most complex challenges, but the key to success is example and persuasion.

References
1   Adair, J. (1983) *Effective Leadership,* Aldershot: Gower
2   Saxe, M. (1757) *Les rêveries ou mémoires sur l'art de guerre,* Jean Drieux.
3   Moran, Lord (1966) *The Anatomy of Courage (Second Edition),* London: Constable.
4   Slim, Field Marshal Sir W. (1957) *Courage and Other Broadcasts,* London: Cassell.
5   Hart, B.L. (1965) *Memoirs Volume 1,* London: Cassell.

Leadership, Teaching and Learning

Philip Hodgson

Author and researcher in the future of leadership
and
Client and Programme Director, Action Learning,
Ashridge Management College

In any discussion about whether leadership can be taught it is important to explore three particular areas: the definition of teaching, the meaning of leadership and the relationship between leadership and learning.

Teaching isn't telling

Whilst many of us will have benefited from good teachers in the past, it is all too easy to fall into an assumption that teaching is in some way linked to 'telling'. If the argument were that you could tell people how to be effective leaders, I would have little hesitation in disagreeing. In my view, leadership teaching has to practise the methods that are most effective in the classroom – harnessing the huge power and opportunity contained within a child's curiosity. The best teachers encourage that curiosity and give it many examples to wonder at, with scarcely ever the need to tell.

Telling people how to lead is roughly equivalent to painting-by-numbers. It produces some kind of result, but is nowhere near as good as 'painting-by-artist'. People who have learned leadership as a series of rules will have an inherent inflexibility that will eventually be their downfall. Leadership skills are learned by example and encouragement rather than by rote of rule.

The meaning of leadership

It is important to pin down just what leadership is. A related question is: where do leaders come from? A review of leadership thinking from the beginning of the twentieth century shows that it has gone through a number of distinct stages.

CLASSIC LEADERS

For the first 50 years of the twentieth century, leadership was what leaders *did*. These 'classic leaders' typically came from a relatively small number of clearly defined places – from particular families, races or castes, through particular education systems, from particular religions, even from particular places. In this era it was easy to select leaders because they came from a particular source.

Around the time of the Second World War the armies of the UK, the USA and Germany all discovered that they were losing their military commanders, many of whom were classic leaders, faster than their classic sources could supply them. Each country independently set up processes to try to understand what effective leaders did and how other people with a high potential to do what leaders did could be identified and developed. In the USA psychologists and other scientists who had carried out this work went into industry and commerce and continued their research projects. From this work came the assessment centre, which today in its refined form is still probably the most effective means of selecting managers and leaders, and predicting potential in those areas. But nothing is completely new – Samuel Pepys thought of a similar idea three centuries ago.

BEHAVIOURAL LEADERS

Out of this work came behavioural leaders. A school emerged which argued that leadership could be described on a map with the two dimensions of concern for people and concern for the task. Attempts were made to chart the most effective styles of leadership on this map. Looking back on this work, we now see it as over simple and failing to allow for the complexity that leadership often assumes, yet it contains many ideas that later became influential in developing leadership thinking.

There was an underlying theme to all the leadership ideas that I have so far described. It was that the role of the leader was to plan, organize and control. The leader had to know at least as much as the 'followers' in order to control what they were doing effectively and to plan for their future work. There was also a big assumption that it was possible to predict and use these predictions as reliable forecasts for what would need to happen next.

VISIONARY LEADERS

Towards the late 1970s and early 1980s in Europe and North America it was becoming clear that it was not always possible to predict accurately, if at all. In addition, many people were uncomfortable about being controlled too firmly or too closely. A new style of leadership was born – visionary leadership. In this new style it was possible to outline your future aim in some graphic and often charismatic way. Visionary leaders sketched a future that followers were naturally drawn towards. The followers had to figure out the details of how to get there, but it was down to the leader to define the ultimate goal. Visionary leadership was about empowerment rather than giving precise instructions.

As we look back on the twentieth century, the classic leader, the behavioural leader and the visionary leader sit alongside each other. One style has not replaced the other. They are not mutually exclusive; they overlap. This can produce confusion about which style is being used by which leader and for which sort of follower. It is no fun being a visionary follower of a leader who wishes mainly to organize and control.

LEADERSHIP IN UNCERTAINTY

What will be the next leadership style? The results of research that my colleagues and I have been conducting over the past 10 years suggest that one of the next important underlying themes for leadership is that of handling the increased uncertainty associated with increased choice. We have studied how leaders get to grips with uncertainty and how that ability has a massive effect on how they can achieve competitive or other kinds of advantage for their organizations.[1]

Leading is learning

A special aspect of learning has emerged strongly from my research. I call it 'difficult learning'. Leaders have to be able to learn and continue to learn through all situations and on all occasions. It is easy to learn the things you are interested in or the things you want to learn, but facing up to some of the hard lessons that our organizations offer us can provide some of the richest and most positive teaching for any leader.

Tackling tasks that are hard and taking on the associated difficult learning is one of the major routes by which individuals become good leaders, and by which good leaders become great leaders. It is tough, particularly when your ideal scheme or pet idea turns out to be wrong. In the commercial world it is easy to get submerged in the trappings of high office and start to believe what everybody else wants to believe about you – which is that you can do it right all the time. Being a great leader while at the same time being vulnerable is a lost skill: it is about not giving up but allowing yourself to have the humility to be able to learn.

If your aim is to be at the front of your market or profession, you and your organization need to be able to do things that your competitors cannot. This means tackling things that are more difficult than those your competitors are prepared to tackle, which requires a revolution in thinking. Facing up to difficult learning involves making public what we don't know, so that we can speed up the search for an answer. For many of us, since school, revealing our lack of knowledge doesn't come easily

So in the long term we are back to schools and to teaching. Can we teach people to take on difficult tasks and thrive doing so? Of course we can. But for the most part that is achieved by encouraging people rather than pressing – pulling rather than pushing.

To conclude, the teacher of leadership has three important responsibilities:

- Teaching by example requires good role models who are worthy of copy.

- Teaching by persuasion must demonstrate that there is a better way that is attractive to the learner.

- Teaching by compulsion often comes from compelling events, by taking the risk of putting learners into a difficult situation so that they can benefit from the difficult learning that ensues.

Reference
1 White, R.P., Hodgson, P. and Crainer, S. (1996) *The Future of Leadership*, London: Pitman; and Hodgson, P. and Crainer, S. (1993) *What Do High Performance Managers Really Do?* London: Pitman.

Developing Leadership Abilities

Adrian Moorhouse, MBE

Director, Lane 4 Management Group
and
Olympic swimming gold medallist

Like General Deverell (see page 119) I believe that leadership can be split into the two areas of task and behaviour, the doing and the being. On the assumption that you can more or less teach many of the mechanics – the task-focused doing – I will focus on three areas. First, is it possible to teach or develop leadership behaviours? Second, is there inborn ability or talent? Third, how does the environment affect development?

Being a former Olympic athlete, I have come from a coaching and developing way of life, and in recent years I have been working in business. In sport, development is long-term, self-owned and achieved within a specific environment. My past life therefore provides a very strong parallel with the business environment. You can teach the mechanics of swimming to anybody, but to make progress you have to coach and develop the skills. At the top are the most successful ones who practise, experience and adapt, and who demonstrate the right behaviour, living the values.

What sort of leadership?
This leads us to the initial questions: What sort of leadership are we talking about? What standard? What level? Are we talking about leadership styles or behaviours for a large majority? Or are we

talking about those at the top? Very few who lead do so in their own right; almost all work for someone who has a responsibility to lead them.

In other words, and in a business context, where does management end and leadership start? Managers do not truly lead. In terms of developing humanistic and affiliative behaviours – the key to effective leadership – the business world is doing extremely well. We are getting very good at encouraging managers to take ownership, encouraging self-awareness and curiosity. Those are developing behaviours, but are they leadership behaviours? In his book, *Principle-Centred Leadership*, Covey[1] states that leadership deals with direction, management with speed; leadership deals with vision, management with maintaining structures.

There are certainly those whose innate abilities will never enable them to reach the standards to fit them for leadership in the more demanding areas. The apprentice who didn't make it at Manchester United (see page 125) may nevertheless have a successful and rewarding career in the first or second division. The middle manager who has a team of 10 sales people is leading them but is perhaps not capable of being the managing director. Leadership behaviours that are developed will be useful but will not make top leaders.

Developing talent

Talent identification and talent development are issues that sport has struggled with for an eternity. In talent identification there is the theory that the best stand out and rise to the top. This leads to the idea of the self-appointed leaders, those who assume the mantle and behave as the leader. Some people shy away from leading and being accountable, but these people do not. Others follow them. Talent development raises the issue of the impact of the environment on development. I remember a sign above the locker room in my university days: 'The aim of this establishment is to create an environment where champions are inevitable.'

Leadership culture

Leaders must be able to develop by using practical application in their own environment. The culture must support the behaviours required, and this is one of the problems. Leaders will come through the ranks of management, yet many of the effective leadership behaviours run counter to good management. Organizations rarely reward risk and opportunism. Training courses teach values that may not exist in the organization. Leadership theories often embody good and bad ways of doing things; rarely do they set the context. Like Olympic champions, leaders will not survive in an environment where they are not supported.

Leadership qualities

It is often possible to develop leadership behaviours – the being. For me these qualities are part of the true leader. General Deverell suggested that some concepts, such as motivation and setting an example, have become unfashionable (see page 121). This may be true, but they are inherent and a necessity for the high achiever. They are like the qualities of an Olympic champion:

- to be willing to learn, even to see failure as a lesson;
- to challenge and yet be prepared to be challenged;
- to listen, listen, listen;
- to have that conviction and self-belief in the value of what you are doing, which is impossible to teach.

The most successful business leaders have these qualities and they have the ability to direct, inspire and communicate them to others. They lead; others follow. True leaders can get motivation from people by inspiring them and communicating what they want and what everybody's part is in achieving a certain goal. The question is whether leaders who know what they want can communicate that right down the organization so that every employee has a motivator and an enthusiasm to be part of that organization's future.

In sport you will find many good leaders who cannot themselves perform the particular activity as well as the people in the
team, but people still respect their wisdom and are led by them. My
swimming coach, whom I greatly respected, was not such a good
swimmer himself, but he had wisdom and knowledge. He could
visualize what I could achieve – he was a good leader.

Reference
1 Covey, S. R. (1991) *Principle-Centred Leadership*, New York: Simon and Schuster.

INFORMATION ON RSA PROGRAMMES

The RSA's programmes focus primarily on business and industry, design and technology, education, the arts and the environment. Projects, which range from campaigns and enquiries, sometimes leading to a publication, to award schemes are largely self-funded with money coming from a variety of sources including trusts, foundations, companies and government. Some projects develop and grow to such an extent as to warrant independent status and they become 'spin-off' organizations. Examples include the RSA Examinations Board, Centre for Tomorrow's Company, Campaign for Learning and National Advisory Council for Careers and Educational Guidance (NACCEG).

Current RSA projects include:

THE ARTS MATTER PROGRAMME

This is a series of projects focused on arts education including:

- The Effect and Effectiveness of Arts Education in Secondary Schools

  A three-year research project with the National Foundation for Educational Research documenting the range of effects and outcomes of a school-based arts education. (Publication: *The Effects and Effectiveness of Arts Education in Schools - NFER, interim report,* 1998

- The Arts in Initial Teacher Training

  A research project documenting and assessing the current situation and future trends with respect to arts experience in the training and development of teachers. (Publication: *The Disappearing Arts?* 1998)

- Arts Audit

  A pilot project developed in Bristol to assist schools in the undertaking of an arts audit. A practical guide is available. (Publication: *Investing in the Arts*, 1998)

- Other arts publications

  Guaranteeing an entitlement to the Arts in schools, 1995; *The Arts Matter* - series of lectures, published by Gower, 1997; *Work, creativity and the arts*, 1999.

Contact: Michaela Crimmin, Head of Arts, RSA

STUDENT DESIGN AWARDS
The Student Design Awards scheme has, over the last 75 years, become the UK's premier competition for student designers, attracting over 3,000 entries a year for over 40 realistic and challenging briefs. The scheme encourages good practice, innovation, sustainability and responsible design solutions. (Publications: *Student Design Awards Projects* book, 1998/99; *Student Design Awards Blueprint Review*, 1997/98; *Design for Ageing Network Teaching Pack*, 1996

Contact: Susan Hewer, Head of Design, RSA

REDEFINING SCHOOLING
This project calls for a re-engineering of the education system as a whole and is working to develop the framework of a new competence-based National Curriculum. It follows on from the recent Redefining Work project, a two-year national debate on how patterns of work are changing and the impact of these changes. (Publications: *Redefining Schooling* discussion paper, 1998; *Redefining Work* report, 1998, available from Gower)

Contact: Lesley James, Head of Education, RSA

PROJECT2001

Project 2001 opens the door to qualifications for people of any age who have built up skills and competencies through experience in the voluntary sector either as volunteers or paid employees. It also offers mentors to managers in participating voluntary organizations. (Publication: *Qualified by Experience*, 1998)

Contact: Janet Fleming, Project Director, Project2001, RSA

FOCUS ON FOOD

This project is run by the RSA at Dean Clough, Halifax. It is a five-year campaign aiming to promote, develop and sustain the place of food in education.

Contact: Anita Cormac, Project Director, Focus on Food, RSA at Dean Clough (tel 01422 250250)

FORUM FOR ETHICS IN THE WORKPLACE

The Forum for Ethics in the Workplace seeks to develop high ethical standards at work. Set up in 1997 and funded by the Comino Foundation, the Forum meets regularly, bringing together a wide variety of professionals to discuss ethics in the context of work.

Contact: Susie Harries, Project Administrator, Forum for Ethics in the Workplace, RSA

OTHER CONTACTS

RSA Examinations Board (OCR)
Tel 01203 470033

The Centre for Tomorrow's Company
Mark Goyder, Director
Centre for Tomorrow's Company
Tel 0171 930 5150

Campaign for Learning
Bill Lucas, Director
Campaign for Learning
Tel 0171 930 1111

National Advisory Council for Careers and Educational Guidance
(NACCEG)
Tel 01962 878340

INDEX

The Arts Matter

The Royal Society for the encouragement of Arts, Manufactures and Commerce

The arts matter to all of us. The arts empower us and give us a vision of what our lives could be; they enable us to understand others; they help us to cross the boundaries of our personalities and social circumstances; they improve creativity, problem-solving and teamworking in business. The arts are an agent of change.

This inspiring and thought-provoking collection of lectures from the RSA's Arts Matter series is a powerful vindication of the value and relevance of the arts in all aspects of our lives from community to workplace. With a specially written introduction by Mark Fisher MP, and opening lecture by the Rt Hon Virginia Bottomley MP, the book presents one of the strongest cases for giving the arts sufficient prominence and influence and offers many proven examples of the dramatic personal and social changes which the arts can facilitate. The lecturers are leading thinkers and practitioners in their fields, ranging from the arts themselves to industry and psychotherapy.

The book includes an agenda for action and will inspire and inform teachers, educationalists and local authorities; policy-makers and lobbyists; community, health and voluntary workers; art administrators and managers; entrepreneurs, employers and middle managers; and practising artists. It is also of great interest to arts tutors and students, charity organisations and corporate sponsorship and PR departments.

Gower

On Community and Environment

A selection of lectures organized by the Royal Society for the encouragement of Arts, Manufactures and Commerce

A thriving society is socially and environmentally self-supporting and sustainable. Locally and globally the same principle applies, and people are increasingly aware of the need to take better care of individuals and their environments.

This book brings together a wealth of positive evidence showing how projects have enabled people to gain a better sense of their community and responsibility for their environment, and suggest ways in which social and environmental problems can be solved.

Sue Clifford, founder director of Common Ground emphasizes the need to 'reconnect' people with their local places and how this can be achieved. Derek Osborn, chairman of the European Environment Agency and of UNED/UK, defines the steps that can move the world forward towards resolving environmental problems and Jonathon Porritt, director of the Forum for the Future, emphasizes the positive signs that our millennium mindsets are gradually shaping up in environmental terms. Other lecturers focus on issues such as volunteering and community action, the role of partnerships and social entrepreneurs in urban regeneration, on volunteering and community action and on housing and architecture.

Gower

On Design and Innovation

A selection of lectures organized by the Royal Society for the encouragement of Arts, Manufactures and Commerce

With the right collaborative and supportive structures the skills and ideas of craftspeople, designers, innovators and scientific researchers can work together to strengthen industry and improve its products. This selection of RSA lectures, which represents the whole creative spectrum from craft and design to scientific invention, describes how this can be done and how these different groups have worked with industry in different ways.

Sir Nicholas Goodison's lecture emphasizes the value of craft skills for industry and outlines ways in which manufacturers can be encouraged to use them more; developing this theme, Robin Levien explains the difference between craft and design skills and how manufacturers can mass produce 'craft magic' to make their products more appealing. The next three lectures show what it is really like to set up creative enterprises (Helen David English Eccentrics, Tomato and Priestman Goode) and stick to one's ideals in the business context. In his lecture about ship container design, naval architect Marshall Meek, Master of the RSA's Faculty of Royal Designers for Industry, describes the realities of working with major shipbuilding companies, balancing the different demands of safety, function and cost, often challenging convention.

The last three lectures in the book focus on scientific research and technological invention. Professor Sir Alec Broers argues that research can no longer be carried out in isolation from the worldwide research network: small groups must collaborate with larger organizations to ensure survival and success – a view echoed in Simon Schaffer's analysis of the decline (and success) of science, and its social and political context. Sir Robert May suggests how the UK's world-class science and engineering base can be better exploited for economic advantage through government and other initiatives so that individual researchers receive proper reward and so that we 'capture the creativity of both individuals and of business'.

Gower